INTRODUCTION TO MUSIC APPRECIATION AND HISTORY

BY

DOROTHY TREMBLE MOYER

FOR THE
DIVISION OF UNIVERSITY EXTENSION
MASSACHUSETTS
DEPARTMENT OF EDUCATION

FOURTH EDITION

1.50

OLIVER DITSON COMPANY
THEODORE PRESSER CO., DISTRIBUTORS
1712 CHESTNUT STREET
· PHILADELPHIA ·

MADE IN U. S. A.

PREFACE TO FIRST EDITION

A noted musical critic and composer recommended recently that people in general study music in the same spirit and from the same point of view as literature is studied. "What would you know of Shakespeare," he asked, "if you had no means of making his acquaintance except at the theatre? How then are you going to know anything of music and musical composers by merely attending a concert or the opera once a season?"

The ability to get the greatest enjoyment out of music is comparatively rare, even among music lovers. Like every other art, music has much which lies below the surface and which can be gained only through study. We have all felt the emotional appeal of music, but only a few of us understand its form and structure and the ideas which underlie it. To give, simply, such an understanding is the purpose of this book.

The development of music from primitive times to the present is here outlined. With a background of the sources from which all musical composition has sprung, the student is given a keener insight into the reasons for a composer's handling his materials as he does. He follows the musical tradition from one period to another, and sees which composers held to the beaten track and which struck out for themselves in new directions, to the advantage or to the detriment of musical progress.

To Mr. Clement Lenom, I wish to extend my heartiest thanks, for without his encouragement this book would not have been written. To Mr. Stuart Mason, also, my gratitude is due for valuable suggestions. I wish to acknowledge also with sincere thanks, the assistance of Miss Mary Terrell, Miss Helen Meinhold, and Mr. Frederick W. Holmes.

THE AUTHOR

PREFACE TO THE FOURTH EDITION

In this edition there have been a number of additions and changes. The lists of phonograph records which are given at the end of each chapter have been brought up to date, those records which are no longer on the market being omitted. To Chapter IX have been added paragraphs on certain musicians whose work has come into greater prominence since the last edition of this book.

There is also a new chapter—a Foreword—which stresses in brief outline those factors which I think are most important for the layman to appreciate in order to achieve a genuine understanding of, and sympathy with, the development of music. No one should become so engrossed in the history of musical forms that he forgets the human impulses that have brought about their evolution. So, as a reminder, I have sketched in this chapter on the "Background of Music" the important influences — geographic, racial, and historic—which have given music its varied characteristics.

THE AUTHOR.

Newton, Mass.
October, 1935.

CONTENTS

v

CONTENTS

A FOREWORD ON THE BACKGROUND OF MUSIC

There are many facets to the study of music. The most obvious which presents itself is the study of an instrument, but there are many other angles which should be considered seriously. There is the study of the science of music which governs the combination of sounds so that they make harmony, and the modelling of that harmony into well-formed structures so that we have variety of musical forms. There is the study of the history of music which records the development of instruments and science. The purpose with which one approaches the study of music depends on whether one is an auditor or performer — professional or amateur. There is, however, one angle which should not be overlooked by any student of music, whatever his status. It is important to realize that music has not grown up "like Topsy" — a separate art arising coincidentally with other arts — but that it is a corporate part of the history of civilization. To separate any of the arts from the social and political currents flowing contemporaneously is to deprive them of the source which gave them life. As the human race progressed, it reached out in ever new directions, seeking gratification of newly unfolding needs and awakening curiosities. Each step taken led inevitably to another step. The sciences and the arts are the incidental outgrowth of mental and physical development. Music, especially, has grown hand in hand with the people of the world.

Perhaps more than any other art, music needs to be seen as a bas-relief against the background of life. It is vitalized by the understanding of the political, social, emotional and intellectual needs which attend its aspect at different periods. These, however, are not the only influences which contributed to the formation of music. Not less important are the contributions of geographical location, and of national characteristics of the individual countries. Just as surely as these two factors create the differences which distinguish the people of one country from those of another, they imprint the music of each country with individual traits. Vast political and social movements have swept many countries simultaneously, but their effect in each country has varied with its individual nature. To understand and enjoy music fully one should have the comprehension of it as the contemporary expression of a people finding their way through the kaleidoscope of life.

Before going on to read the ensuing chapters in this brief history of music, let us consider the three factors which form the background of music.

First, the permanent factor of geographical location, and climate. Those countries in the temperate zones, as France and Germany, have a normal climate, and fertile soil rich in natural resources. The people are busy with a life well-balanced between play and work. In the southern climes, as in Italy, there is an over-amount of heat, but still these countries have rich soil. In the northern countries, as the Scandinavian, conditions of living are far different. The climate inclines to be cold, and one finds the long winters of the Land of the Midnight Sun. The countryside is more barren, and it requires grim determination and indomitable courage to wrest a living from these lands. These are the unalterable elements of geography and climate.

Second, are the semi-permanent factors of race — the people. These are affected by migrations and inter-blending, but there are fundamental characteristics which we associate with different nationalities.

The Germans are industrious, serious, keenly artistic. Their country is rich in folk-lore and legends. Every ivy-shrouded view is haunted by a romantic tale. The Rhine whispers of the Rhine-maidens who guarded the gold of the Nibelung, and bears upon its breast the ghost of Lohengrin and his knightly swan. Birds whistling through the forests bring memories of Siegfried who followed the song of a bird to the sleeping Brünnhilde, where she lay on her stone couch surrounded by darting flames. Fertile valleys, rugged mountains, stalwart forests make Germany a beautiful country. The German music is like the soil from which it springs, rich and sturdy, but ever melodic in beauty.

Not less serious are the French people, but their earnestness is perhaps not so obvious. They are vivacious and imaginative. The country perhaps has not majesty, but it has homely charm. Picture the golden wheat fields in which bloom the red poppy and the bluet; the thatched roofed cottages over which roses run riot; the lazy rivers winding beneath bending trees; the orderly vegetable gardens, olive groves, and vineyards. French music combines melody with a marked rhythm, and a warm supporting harmony. These people have never been contented with merely pleasant sounds, or cold intellectual compositions. They must have atmosphere, picturesqueness in their music. They refuse to think abstractly.

In sunny Italy, with its breath-taking beauty of lakes, mountains and sea, we find a natural gift for melody. The disposition of the people is imbued with the sunniness of the climate; their liquid language is incapable of a harsh sound. Even a newsboy crying his wares sounds as if he were repeating a musical phrase, a sound quite different from the "uxtra" we are accustomed to hear. From this country has come some of the greatest vocal music.

And now in the Scandinavian countries — Norway, Sweden, Denmark — and in Finland, the farthest north, what do we find? The Land of the Midnight Sun; the stark beauty of barren mountains gashed by a cutting sea; the bleakness of long dark winters; the mirth and merry-making of short summers. Superstitions and mythological lore dating from the earliest days are still to be found here. Austere beauty, solitude and the hardships of a rigorous climate have given the northern countries simplicity in living which is underlaid by a quality of wistfulness, and mystery. All these color the music of these countries. Inclined to the minor key, it is at times gay, at times sad, or dramatic, and it is always vital.

Russia, because of her great size, has the harshness of the cold north and the mellowness of the warm south. This is a country of extremes where can be found the highest education and the lowest illiteracy; great luxury and primitive squalor. Numerous races have been assimilated to make the Russian people: Mongolian, Arabic, Gothic, Jewish, and many others. From this mixture comes music which is virile, brilliant, gay, melancholy. Pagan superstitions and fervid religious faith are voiced in the compositions of Russia.

In the British Isles there are a variety of types of people, and the music differs according to their characteristics. The English are a simple, wholehearted race living a healthly out-door life. Their music is full of a robust, hearty spirit. The Gaelic Music of Ireland, Scotland and Wales has a marked rhythm which bears some similarity to syncopation. The Irish is filled with merriment, and lilting tenderness; but the Scotch is tinged with the soberness and melancholy of the far north. The Celts have a firm belief in fairies and evil spirits, and one finds mystery and haunting wistfulness in their rich, beautiful music.

Lastly we consider America. This is too vast a country to characterize. There are too many different physical aspects, too many dissimilar races represented, to select a type. Manifold occupations, interests and racial backgrounds find expression in American music. As the country grows older, fusion will gradually take place, and there will become established a type of music which will bear the unmistakable stamp of the American people.

Third, we now come to the final factor in the background of music: the evolutionary one of history, events, movements. Each epoch has had its own needs and interests which were expressed in the art of the period. Let us run quickly through the centuries.

In Ancient times men were primarily concerned with the bare matters of existence, but even primitive man chanted his prayers to his gods. As races grew, and means of living improved, culture also developed. With the age of the Greeks we find a high stage of culture, but music was still largely rhythmical.

After the Fall of Rome begin the Middle Ages which may be roughly said to extend to the 13th Century. The Medieval period is a colorful one in which the world began to emerge into its adolescence. Men were finding their way out of the dark clouds of pagan superstitions into the light of Christianity. Philosophy, matters of general education became their concern. Likewise, races began to segregate into sections out of which finally grew the nations of the world. Tremendous wars were fought in the effort to establish boundaries. (In some of these wars may be found the roots of present international problems.)

As the grip of Christianity became stronger, religious wars were fought. Out of this age there comes to us some of the most beautiful literature of all times: the Arthurian Legend, the Parsifal Legend; the Nibelungen Lied; the Charlemagne epic of France — the Chanson de Roland. The minstrels who contributed to these legends added the gift of melody to musical rhythm. Let no one call the Medieval Period dark; it is the rich, colorful, sincere struggle of Man toward enlightenment.

This earnest seeking brought about, inevitably, the periods of the Renaissance and Reformation. In the 13th Century people began to be less interested in philosophy, and more curious about more practical matters. This awakening is first noticed in Italy, and from this country it was to spread far. Scientific theories were evolved: such as astronomy, the shape of the world. Inventions which made travel and discovery of greater ease were studied, for instance, the compass. The 16th Century found the secular interests of the Renaissance at their height. Wealth, power, luxuries — all material things — were avidly sought. Some of the greatest art came into existence at this time. Look back over the years of the Renaissance and you will find the names of Dante — who opened the gate into the new era — and later those of Machiavelli, the Borgias, the Medici, da Vinci, Michelangelo, Cellini, and others whose names conjure up visions of beauty, cruelty, skill.

A parallel current to the secularism of the Renaissance was the religious one of the Reformation. This was a natural protest against the vices which arose from setting too high a value on worldly things. There were precursors of this moment in England and France as early as the 15th Century, but in Germany in the 16th Century, it became a revolutionary affair with far-reaching results. The effort to reform abuses in the Church led to the establishment of the Protestant Church, and the counter-reformation within the Catholic Church.

How was music affected by the changes which took place during this era of three or four hundred years? The curiosity which guided investigation into every channel of thought was directed toward musical instruments. Old types were improved and new ones were invented. The countries interested in the Renaissance encouraged the writing of secular music for amusement and entertainment. Those people who were concerned with the Reformation sought new music to be used in churches and to embody the new religious emotions. So, not only were there two trends of thought which gripped the world, but there were also two distinct trends in the composition of music.

The emotional fervor of this long period of time settled down into the calm of the latter 17th Century, and 18th Century. The inventions begun in the preceding period were carried to far greater improvements. Medicine, machinery — the whole field of science opened out to illimitable extents. The trend now was toward the exclusively intellectual; the formalism of the classical 18th Century. During this time, rigid standards in letters, art, architecture and music were raised and adhered to by all. Individualism, personal expression, were anathema. This cold was shattered by the fires of Revolution in France which, fanned by Napoleon, threatened to sweep across all Europe. The intense fervor of patriotism broke down reserves of self-control, and emotions sought relief in poetry, revived folk-lore, simple song melodies. The Romantic period of the 19th Century produced a wealth of dramatic and lyrical music which holds the love of every music listener today.

At last we come to the 20th Century. With its unsettled political conditions, its perfection in machinery which is substituted for man-power, its advancements in Science; with its haste and speed, its feverish unrest, its constant pushing on to new fields of effort, this century has produced what is called "modernism" in all branches of art. There are individuals who are not disciples of this new trend, but many have introduced, and experimented with innovations that are not always given a warm reception. However, whether we understand or like a new experiment we can examine it and feel interest in it as another evidence of its era.

So, bearing in mind the background which is so important to music, let us proceed to the history of its development.

Introduction to Music Appreciation and History

CHAPTER I

THE THREE FUNDAMENTALS

Hundreds of years ago the Crusading armies, as they lay camped at evening before the walls of Jerusalem, whiled away their time with songs. One tune in particular was a favorite. It was simple and brief; yet something in its healthy, vigorous spirit caught and held the interest of the Crusaders. In France this tune is known as *Chanson de Malbrouk*, the popular song which recounts the story of Malbrouk going to war. Today, after nearly eight centuries, we still sing that same tune—to the words, *We won't go home until morning.**

The modern concert program never contains that title; but the tune still lives notwithstanding. Even if we think it a little undignified, we like it. And certainly music that has endured so long must have in it some of the elements of greatness. What, then, are the qualities that give permanence to music? Are they common to all good music? Do they exist both in the jolly old Crusade tune and in the Beethoven symphonies? In this chapter we shall find the answers to those questions, and by doing so we shall learn at least a little about *how to listen to music.*

From the earliest period of which history gives us any record, there was never a time when man did not have some sort of instinct for music. We may easily imagine that almost as soon as human beings started to develop language for the expression of their ideas, they also began to use music for the expression of their emotions. And just as the language of today began with very simple forms, so the highly developed music of today took its origin from music of a cruder, more primitive sort. Since that beginning music has progressed marvelously, taking to itself from time to time new principles and refinements. But no great principle has ever been lost or displaced. Though the modern orchestral work appeals to its audience in a far greater variety

*See *Introduction to Study of National Music* by Carl Engel, page 190.

1

of ways than primitive music appealed to its half-savage hearers, it contains none the less that very element of appeal which stirred the ancient tribesmen to frenzied enjoyment. In music the present and the past have much in common, and it is for that reason that our first step in studying how to appreciate music will be to find out something about its growth.

Among the earliest peoples music appeared in a form that would seem to us very incomplete—even unmusical. The chief, and often the sole, instruments used were rude drums, on which the player thumped with his fingers. Of course such instruments could not produce anything like tunes; but in one respect they were musical for the player in his thumping made some strokes, or beats, longer and some stronger than others, according to a definite plan. For instance, in every group of four beats he might make the first two weak and short and the last two long and emphatic; or in a group of two beats equal in length he might make the first strong and the second weak. In short, he arranged the beats according to rhythm. Now while this music of monotonous but rhythmic beats may not have been beautiful, it exerted a decided power over its hearers. They danced to it; indeed, if the rhythm was strong enough, they probably could not have helped dancing to it whether they wanted to or not, for rhythm more than any other quality in art is almost instinctive. Even to-day, after centuries of civilization we yield to it almost as readily as did the savage. When we hear music with a "good swing to it," we feel the strong desire to follow it by some bodily motion—by dancing, by waving a finger, or by swaying the head. The savage then with his uncouth drum laid the first stone in the foundation of music; he established the enduring principle of *rhythm*.

The second stage in musical development dates from the time when man, perhaps through listening to bird songs or more probably through experiment with his own voice, noticed that some tones are higher than others and some are lower. For a long time before that he had shouted in triumph or rage, he had wailed, he had groaned; but never with any conscious attention to tone. Now he began to arrange different tones in succession—a high tone, a low tone, one lower still, then a higher one. In course of time he came to make and remember tunes. This new kind of music too he used to express emotions, but not the almost purely physical emotions he had expressed by rhythm. Tune he used for the more spiritual emotions, such as grief, happiness and love. Then presently he began to combine *tune* and *rhythm;* and music approached more nearly to its present state.

Finally, as man developed intellectually he acquired the habit of putting things together according to a regular pattern, and of making adjustments and variations in the materials with which he worked. Seizing upon the simple rhythmic tune he made little changes in it; first sang it one way, then in a slightly different way; then combined several varied forms of the tune and sang them in succession as one song. And in doing so, he gave to music its third great principle—*structure.*

So much for the gradual development of rhythm, tune and structure—*the three fundamental qualities of music.* Let us see how they apply in particular cases. To begin with take the *Crusade song* which we have already mentioned; and notice its strongly marked rhythm. If you sing the modern words you will find that in the first part of the song the strong beats fall on the words "won't" and "home" and on the first syllable of "morning."

We Won't Go Home Until Morning

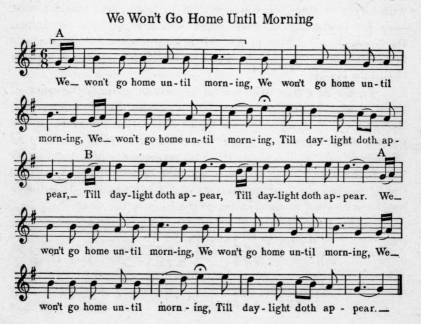

The shorter and weaker beats are so arranged as to give a lurching swing, which is easy to follow.

As for the element of tune, we shall discover nothing elaborate, yet such tune as there is possesses one important quality, namely, the quality of being easily remembered. Combined with the rhythm the tune expresses quite perfectly a strong, joyous mood, which is the purpose of the song.

Now for the structure. If you will again sing or play over the song, you will recognize that the main theme is introduced in the first nine notes marked A, and is repeated twice in slightly altered form, with a few notes added to form a conclusion. This is the first part of the song. The second part beginning at B, consists of a new tune, pitched higher, but still clearly related by its rhythm to the original tune. A single repetition of the new tune completes the second part of the song. The third part, also marked A, consists merely of an exact repetition of the first part. We have, then, a simple structure of three parts.

Not only here but in all other good music *repetition,* as we have seen, *is a fundamental principle of musical construction.* Just as in the *Crusade song,* the first nine notes are repeated with slight changes, so you will find in most great masterpieces, near the beginning, a brief theme which will recur throughout the composition. This theme conveys the composer's message to his audience. The various ways in which he repeats it express changing moods.

To see how this principle of repetition governs the work of great music builders, let us now consider Beethoven's *Fifth Symphony.* A symphony is a long composition of several movements, each movement being made up of several parts. In Beethoven's *Fifth Symphony* these movements are held together by a common theme. The first four notes constitute the tie which binds together the four movements of the symphony. This theme has been likened to the "knock of Fate upon the door."

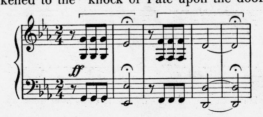

The theme begins in a measured, solemn manner and is repeated in the second group of four notes. Then it is picked up briskly and repeated with slight changes until the audience is thoroughly familiar with it.

Soon comes the repetition of the theme, clearly and boldly.

And almost immediately follows a new passage of theme development.

Here, in the last two measures of this selection, we again have part of the theme.

Here we have the theme almost as it appeared in the second example from this symphony:

Near the conclusion of the first movement, from which all of the foregoing examples have been taken, we have the "knocking of fate" in this form:

In the third movement, the Scherzo, the theme enters brazenly, after a very soft passage. Here the "knocking of fate" idea is still preserved, as indicated thus: [＿＿＿] ; but this time it is in ¾ rhythm.

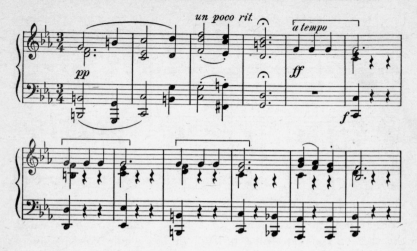

Later it merely whispers:

In the last movement we have the rhythm of the theme thus disguised:

Then again we hear it coming in very timidly:

The structure of this symphony is thus based on a carefully worked pattern—fascinating to follow. Once you have caught the theme, you can trace it through the whole composition in varied moods and forms. And whereas the structure of the *Crusade Song* was so simple that it could be grasped almost without conscious effort, the structure of the *Fifth Symphony* is so full of ingenious, unexpected developments that it affords to the hearer an interest additional to the interest of rhythm and tune.

With regard to the latter two qualities we need say very little. It is obvious at once that in Beethoven's *Fifth Symphony* they are excellent. The rhythm is pronounced; the tune, though brief, has in it a solemnity that is clearly the expression of a spiritual emotion.

Consider now that the *Symphony*, which is strong in rhythm, tune and structure, is great; while the *Crusade Song*, depending for its effect chiefly on rhythm, is by comparison much inferior. A little thought will make clear not only why that is true, but also how we may judge the real worth of other music. Rhythm, tune and structure in music, as we have seen, are suitable for expressing the three great characteristics of man—body, mind and spirit. And as the greatness of man depends upon the development of all these characteristics, the greatness of music depends upon its power to express them all in their highest form. Comparatively little music ever succeeds in doing that. Some compositions, though fairly well developed on all three sides—physical, mental and spiritual—fall short of greatness because they do not express anything that is really fine; the rhythm is erratic or unnatural; the tune appeals only to sickly sentiment; the structure, or pattern, is commonplace or feeble. Other compositions show a one-sided development, depending for their popularity on rhythm alone. In the latter class belongs most of our so-called "jazzy" music, which has little to offer except rhythm. So long as one is content to dance, to the exclusion of spiritual and intellectual activity, such music satisfies—but only so long. Thirty years ago, on the other hand, our popular music was lopsided in the direction of tune; its rhythm was not highly developed, and its structure was as uninteresting as the structure of popular music today.

Truly great music, however, is never without something worth while in the way of structure. At a good concert, almost without exception, every piece of music that you hear played will be based on the repetition, in various forms, of a theme. And the right way to listen to good music, for greatest enjoyment, is to notice the theme as you hear it early in the composition and then to follow it, recognizing it in the different forms which it assumes. After a little practice, you will have no difficulty in thus tracing the composer's theme idea from the beginning of a work to the end. By doing so you will add greatly to your enjoyment and appreciation of music.

The following phonograph records may be used to illustrate some of the musical selections in this chapter.

Title	Victor Record No.
FIFTH SYMPHONY (Beethoven) Royal Albert Hall Orchestra.	9029-9032
SPRING SONG (Mendelssohn) Renée Chemet (violin.)	1242
HUMORESQUE (Dvořák) Fritz Kreisler (violin.)	6692
MY OLD KENTUCKY HOME (Foster) Rosa Ponselle.	6509
BATTLE HYMN OF THE REPUBLIC, Victor Band.	21841
DRINK TO ME ONLY WITH THINE EYES, Tibbett.	1238
OVER THERE (George M. Cohan) Victor Band.	35937
DUKE OF MARLBOROUGH, Victor Male Chorus.	20152

QUESTIONS

1. What do we mean by the *theme* of a composition?

2. What important principle governs the *development* of the theme?

3. Name the three fundamental qualities of every musical composition.

4. Tell briefly how you would distinguish between good music and poor music.

5. Tell concisely what you have learned from this chapter about how to listen to music.

6. Select from the list below two compositions with which you are acquainted and criticise each according to the following three points.
   (a)   Has it an interesting rhythm?
   (b)   Has it a good tune?
   (c)   Do you think it has qualities which will give it a permanent place in the field of good music?

Mendelssohn's *Spring Song*
Over There
Which Hazel
Drink To Me Only With Thine Eyes

My Old Kentucky Home
Dvořák's *Humoresque*
The Battle Hymn of the Republic
Hello, Frisco

Chapter II

PRIMITIVE MUSIC

Music has been broadly defined by Fétis as "the art of moving the feelings by combinations of sound;" and taken in this broad sense music may be considered as having originated with the first members of the human race. Certainly there is no other fine art which reflects the activity of the spirit more perfectly than does music. Every great period of mental strength has been accompanied by a corresponding term of activity in music.

For much of our information regarding the music of ancient times, we have to depend on the rude pictures left by primitive man, and on legends. But we know that music is as old as mankind. Musical instruments, used by the cave men even, have been found.

The earliest advanced civilization from which any coherent traces of music have come down to us, was developed along the Nile. We obtain a great part of our information about the

EGYPTIAN HARP

music of Egypt from a curious source. The Egyptians deposited their mummies in tombs of great size. The walls of these tombs were covered with pictures, the subjects of which embraced the entire range of the public and domestic life of these people. Since many were musicians we have learned from these pictures what instruments the Egyptians used. The favorite one was the harp.

The Egyptians employed music united with poetry and pantomimic dancing as a feature of religious ceremonies, as a social diversion, and as a courtly luxury. They had choruses, which were accompanied by clapping of the hands to beat out the rhythm. All the princely households appear to have had their regular staff

11

of musicians, while the people of lower social grade had to be content with the temporary services of street musicians, who played and sang and danced for all festivities. These public musicians also undertook the entire contract of mourning for the dead, even to the extent of producing a small vial of tears.

One of the earliest songs of Egypt was the song of Maneros, whose father was the first king of Egypt. Maneros died at a very early age, and in his honor a song of mourning was composed that bewailed the coming of Death to Youth. Later this same song was used to warn the thoughtless that sooner or later they too must die. At banquets the small figure of a corpse was passed among the guests while the musicians sang the song of Maneros. The guests were warned that they should "eat, drink, and be merry" for tomorrow they might be as the corpse upon which they were looking.

Egypt had schools where music was taught. The lessons were oral, for none of the music was written down. The Egyptian system of music was, however, well developed and was the fountainhead of some of our musical ideas.

The following is an example of Egyptian music as it is sung today.

Egyptian Love Song

Doos yá lel - lee; Doos yá lel - lee;— Doos yá lel - lee; Doos yá lel - lee;— Doos yá lel - lee; Doos yá le - lee; 'Esh-ke mah-boo-bee fe - ten - nee.

Even today the Egyptians sing while they work. For instance, the sailors on a ship have a certain song which they sing when departing on a voyage, and another which they sing when they return safely home. If perchance, during the voyage they are about to collide with another ship, they sing a song while trying

*See *Music of the Most Ancient Nations* (second edition) by Carl Engel, page 260.

HEBREW PSALTERY

to avert the disaster, and if their efforts are successful there is still another song which they sing as they pass safely by.

The Hebrews, who come second in point of musical antiquity, derived most of their knowledge of music from the Egyptians. David was responsible for the greatest step in the progress of Hebrew music. In 520 B. C. the custom was introduced into the temples of singing to the accompaniment of instruments, among which the triangular harp and the psaltery—a square harp-like affair—were prominent.

The Psalms were collected for this purpose, and never had a church so grand a body of poetry as that of the Hebrews. They had a method of responsive service which is still used today. One Hebrew melody still in modern use, but said to have been sung by Miriam and her companions after the deliverance from Pharaoh's host, is called *Song of Moses* and is quoted here.

Song of Moses *

Az ya-shir Mo-she ub - ne— yis ra - el et ha-shi-ra ha zot— la - do - nai— va yo-me-ru le - mor. A - do - nai ish mil cha - ma A - do - nai— she - mo mai-ke bot Par-ngho ve- che - lo ya - ra— ba - yam u - mib- char - sha-li shav— tu-beng - u— be yam suf.

*See *Music of the Most Ancient Nations* (second edition) by Carl Engel, page 327.

Louis C. Elson in his *Curiosities of Music* tells us that "in the Talmud there is mention of an organ which had but ten pipes, yet gave one hundred different tones. This instrument is placed about the beginning of the Christian Era, and is called 'Magrepha'. It is said its tones were so powerful that when it was played, the people in Jerusalem could not hear each other talk."*

Next we come to Greece. Here still we find the Egyptian influence. Pythagoras, who was born about 580 B. C., spent twenty-eight years in Egypt and there learned much of musical science. He built a musical scale which has been only slightly altered to form our present scale.

In studying the history of Grecian music we find for the first time that the bard—the wandering minstrel—had become an important factor in the development of music. The Homeric poems, of which everyone knows, were chanted by traveling minstrels called Rhapsodists, to the accompaniment of the *cithara* or the *lyre*, both of which were characteristic Greek forms of the harp.

GREEK LYRE

GREEK FIGURE WITH LYRE

In the *Odyssey* we find passages which prove that the bard was an honored guest in any company, ready at call to entertain by singing.

*See *Music of the Most Ancient Nations* by Carl Engel, pages 296 and 297.

It was in Greece that the art of chorus singing was first greatly cultivated. The leader improvised rhapsodies upon various topics, and the chorus came in with the refrain whenever the soloist needed repose from lack of breath or of inspiration. Out of this custom gradually grew a kind of lyric drama.

The Greeks also had musical contests in which the prize seems to have gone to the one who made the most noise rather than to him who played with the most expression. There is a story told of one member of a contest who blew his trumpet with such great force (knowing the louder he blew the greater his chance of winning favor) that he broke a blood vessel and fell dead on the spot. An example of music probably more tuneful than that of the ill-fated trumpeter is quoted in the following example.

A Pythian Ode *

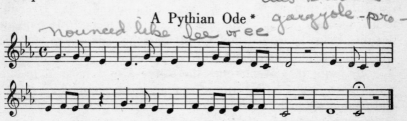

In the music of Rome, we find the Greek influence clearly apparent. After the conquest of Greece by the Romans, Greek music received a new impetus on Roman soil through the performance of Greek slave-musicians for their masters. But unfortunately Rome was too well content to accept music as a feature of the service expected of slaves, and it added almost nothing original to musical development. Indeed the Romans hardly regarded music as an art to be enjoyed for its own sake. To them it was useful principally as an added attraction to the spectacular games and dramatic performances which they so enjoyed. It contributed an inspiration to their dances, and it played an important part in helping them to develop the art of pantomime. But the Romans were not a musical people in the deeper sense of the word.

Of all the Roman emperors none showed a stronger fancy for music than Nero. He studied the art intensively and was very fond of performing in public. He took part in all the contests,

*See *History of Music*, Volume I, by Naumann, page 140.

where of course the prize was invariably awarded to him from motives of prudence on the part of the judges. Many of his songs lasted from morning to night. After beginning to sing he would pause only for an occasional glass of water. By the way, Nero did not "fiddle while Rome burned"; he sang.

In striking contrast to the indolent attitude of the Romans toward music is that of the early Hindoos, who attributed to it a divine origin. Each note of their musical scale was named after a nymph, and music in general they considered as having more than earthly power. Some modes, according to their legends, were never to be sung by mortal man, for they believed that any singer who should attempt them would be consumed by the fire of his song.

A story is told of one poor singer who was commanded by the Ruler to sing the *Raagni of Fire*. He plunged into a river up to his neck and sang. Soon the water began to boil, he paused, but the Ruler demanded the rest of the song, and at the end the singer burst into flames and was consumed.

In India in ancient times there was also a musical drama which possessed certain traits in common with the modern opera, and the natives had a musical instrument invented about 5000 B. C.* called the "ravanostron," which was, in very primitive form, the ancestor of the violin.

This is an example of Hindoo music as given in Hamilton's *Outlines of Musical History*, page 11.

From a Melody of India

Japan and China also had music in prehistoric times, but because of their conservatism they have since made slow progress. Their music was symbolic of all that was best and beauti-

*See *A Popular History of Music* by W. S. B. Mathews, page 70.

ful, and they have been reluctant to accept music not created with the same symbolic purpose.

A *Japanese Air* and *A Song of Chinese Rowers* are given in the following examples:

Japanese Air *

> He to tsu to yah_____ He____ to yo a ka de ba,
>
> Nek hee ya ka dé   Nek hee ya ta dé   Ka___ za du
>
> ta te ta ru Ma-tsu ka za du,___ _Ma-tsu ka za du!

Song of Chinese Rowers †

Solo by Master

Chorus by Crew

Thus we find that music has always been an integral part of the life of man. Even the most primitive people found in it a satisfying mode of self-expression. Their music was closely connected with their religion, and indeed has always been with all people a means by which man has expressed worship of his God.

In the next chapter we shall take up the minstrel, direct descendant in art of the Grecian bard, who sang his way through the land, spreading tales of love and heroism. It was this type of musician who did most for the development of music in the Middle Ages, and his songs echo in our ears today.

The following phonograph record may be used to illustrate musical selections in this chapter.

Title	Victor Record No.
HYMN TO APOLLO (composed 287 B. C.)—Palestrina Choir.	20896

*See *Music of the Most Ancient Nations* (second edition) by Carl Engel, page 139.
†See *Introduction to Study of National Music* by Carl Engel, page 114.

QUESTIONS

1. How did the early Egyptian musicians provide for rhythm?

2. State the probable source of early Hebrew music.

3. State briefly the historical origin of the musical scale.

4. What was the contribution of the Greeks to musical development?

5. What can be said critically of Roman music in ancient times?

6. What was the contribution of India in the way of musical instruments?

CHAPTER III

FOLKSONGS OF THE MIDDLE AGES

A noted author, Theodore Storm, has described folksongs in language that is worth remembering. "Folksongs," he says, "are not made at all; they grow, they fall from the clouds, they fly over the country like gossamer, here and there, and are sung at a thousand places at once. We find our own doings and sorrows in these songs. It seems as if we had all helped to make them." In plainer speech, a folksong is the work not of one man but of a tribe, a nation, a race. We cannot trace it to a single composer. All that we know of its origin is that for centuries people have sung it. What voice gave it to the world, in what village it first was heard—these are questions for which history has no answer.

The folksong is the wild flower of music in contrast to the composed song or garden flower. Since it springs from the soil it naturally has a native tang of peculiar charm. The preservation of these traditional songs is a matter of great importance for under modern conditions they are dying out, yet only in recent years has any systematic attempt been made to record them. It is an interesting fact that Mr. Cecil Sharp, the eminent English authority, found early British folksongs in their greatest purity among the primitive whites in the mountain districts of North and South Carolina.

Perhaps the greatest quality in folk music is that it expresses very perfectly the emotions and the experiences of the people among whom it originated. There is a very good reason for that —a reason at which we have just hinted, namely, that no man ever created a folksong in its final form. For while the original tune may have been suggested by a minstrel, it was altered in some way by almost everyone who sang it, as it traveled from place to place—never written down, always passed from mouth to mouth, like a superstition or a fairy tale. There were no music copyrights in those days. Each man sang it as he liked. And so, gradually, with a change here and a change there, it was shaped to suit the taste and to express the emotions of a whole people or sometimes of a whole race.

Then, too, it survived only because it expressed the feelings common to everybody. It took its subject matter from tradition

19

—from fragments of great poetry, from love stories, from the personal experiences of its originator, and from legends centering about the deeds of great heroes.   The following melody, one of the oldest that has been preserved to us from early European music, was written in praise of Charlemagne during the same year that he died.*

The music of Britain and of Western Europe comes home very close to us, and it is that music which we shall principally consider.   By the early part of the eleventh century, Europe had

FIFTEENTH CENTURY MINSTRELS PLAYING THE HARP, FLUTE, PIPE AND TABOR

an abundance of folk tunes; and as means of travel improved, men going from one place to another carried their music with them.   During this time there were groups of professional mu-

*See *History of Music*, Vol I, by Naumann, page 199.

sicians who made their living by journeying from town to town and from one country to another, singing in exchange for food and shelter. These strolling singers played an important part in the development of music, for they devoted their lives to the serious study of musical art.

In a general way, these traveling musicians were much alike through Europe. The subjects on which they sang were generally similar; their instruments, although some were in the form of a harp and some were more like the violin, all had this point in common: they were easily portable and usually quite simple in form. But in different countries the strolling singers went under different names, and acquired local characteristics.

With the coming of the professional musician, too, the practice of writing down music became more and more general, but it was during later centuries that our present system of written music gradually came into being. For instance, the melody which we would now set down in this form:

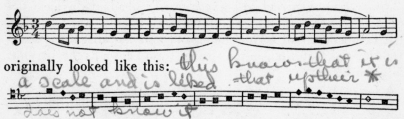

originally looked like this:

This old melody, *When the nightingale shall sing** (*Quant li Rosignol jolis*), is by Regnault, Châtelain de Coucy, a gallant troubadour who accompanied Richard the Lion-hearted in one of his crusades to Palestine and died there in 1192. A French poem written about 1228 tells how the dying troubadour requested that his heart be embalmed and sent to his lady-love.

The Troubadours of France brought vast improvement to music. Often of noble birth, they sang of those subjects most interesting to the people........war, politics and courtly love. To appreciate the love songs of that period, we must bear in mind that the Knight of those days observed a strict etiquette in his love-making. He was humble and devoted to the lady of his choice, and he honored her by long, patient service that was almost

*This song is given in full in *One Hundred Folksongs of all Nations* (Bantock) in The Musicians Library.

worship.   That service was wholly voluntary, and if the lady did not reward it by kindness, the lover might plead—he might sigh—but never reproach.   The courtly lover endowed his lady with all the virtues, and in his songs he celebrated them.   But never did he reveal the lady's name; she was too sacred to be mentioned personally in public.   Into these love songs the Troubadours poured their individuality.   Just as each thought his lady the loveliest in all the land, so he felt that his songs to be worthy of her must be the finest yet composed.   Indeed so worshipful in spirit was the music of these Troubadours that many of their songs have since been converted into sacred music by the mere change of a word or two in text.

The same effort toward originality was not made in the political songs.   Often the Troubadour was content to compose the words of such songs and fit them to tunes already written.   But the words in themselves were frequently clever, with a strong vein of shrewd satire running through them.   Occasionally debates even were carried on between two Troubadours by means of political songs.   If subjects of political interest were wanting, the Troubadour had no objection to turning moralist for a while.   One song of that kind, in the special form known as the *sirvente*, is given here:

The words of this sirvente cannot be translated literally but you can get the meaning from the following:

I wish to begin a new sirvente, that which I will say on Judgment Day to Him who will draw me up from nothingness.   If He wishes to chastise me for my sins, and if He casts my soul to the devils, I will say, "O Lord, pity I claim, I have suffered harshly on earth.   Preserve me, please, from torment."

But the Troubadours and the Trouvères, who were practically the Troubadours of northern France, won great popularity by their singing of stories and rhymed novels. Especially the narrative of *Aucassin and Nicolette,* two lovers who were united after much hardship and cruel separation, delighted both court and countryside. Indeed to this very day the French people think of Aucassin and Nicolette as the ideal types of faithful lovers, and during the late war many French soldiers wore good

Aucassin and Nicolette

*Music arranged from the old music by Horace Mansion; and words translated from the Old French by Michael West. A simple kind of harmony began to appear in the time of Charlemagne.

luck charms representing the hero and the heroine of that old love
story. One of the prettiest incidents in the romance of Aucassin
and Nicolette is described in the preceding song with music and
words.

In that part of the story immediately preceding the song,
Nicolette had escaped from the tower where she was imprisoned,

and finding herself at nightfall in the forest, had built herself an arbor of boughs and vines. When it was completed she thought, "If Aucassin really loves me, he is searching for me now, he will come to this arbor, and if his love is true, he will know that it is mine." So she decided to hide under some nearby bushes to watch for his approach. And, indeed, Aucassin was searching for her, and did come to the arbor, and, on seeing it, did declare that no other hands than those of Nicolette could have built anything so lovely. He concluded to pass the night there, happy in the thought that Nicolette could not be far away and that he would find her on the morrow. As he lay down to rest he saw a clear, bright star, and gazing upon it he sang.

When the song was ended Nicolette, convinced by its tenderness that Aucassin's love was true, left her hidingplace and went to him.

Still another part of the story, in which Nicolette disguises herself as a Troubadour and journeys—unchallenged and unafraid—through foreign lands and camps of war, shows us how cordially the Troubadours were welcomed wherever they cared to go. They alone could enter "where angels feared to tread."

It may have been from such song-stories as *Aucassin and Nicolette* that Adam de la Halle, one of the most celebrated Trouvères, got the idea for his musical play, *Le jeu de Robin et Marion,* which he produced before the King of Naples at about the year 1285. This was probably the first step in the development of opera. One of the songs from that play is given here. It is called *Robin Loves Me.*

Robin Loves Me

*From *Troubadour Songs* compiled and arranged by Clarence Dickinson. Copyrighted by H. W. Gray Company; and published here with permission.

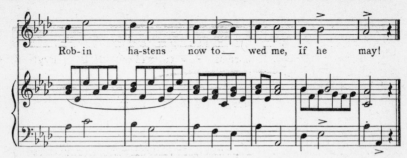

Rob-in   ha-stens   now to__ wed me, if he   may!

Shortly after the time of Adam de la Halle, the great wars which swept Europe practically destroyed the Troubadours, much to the detriment of musical progress.

THE MINNESINGERS

In Germany the Minnesingers corresponded very closely to the Troubadours, but the Mastersingers introduced into musical history a new ideal. Recruited mostly from among the burgers and tradespeople they approached music as a craft, like silver-working or stone-cutting. They organized into guilds—medieval forms of trade union—to which candidates could be admitted only by competitive examination, and to which no one could be admitted as a master unless he invented some new style of rhyme. The Mastersinger thus was really a master workman in music. The fame of one such master, Hans Sachs, by trade a shoemaker, has been handed down to us in Wagner's opera *Die Meistersinger von Nürnberg*.

In England, Ireland and Scotland the popular love for music dates back many centuries. A legend has come down to us which records a great triumph of music in Ireland as early as 365 B. C. A young prince, it seems, had been beaten by his enemies and had been obliged to leave his throne in the possession of a usurper. Defeated and discouraged, he was on the point of giving up his claim to rule, when his betrothed led before him a celebrated band of musicians and had them sing to him a song which she had composed. Inspired by its sentiments he roused himself to new effort and succeeded finally in driving the usurper from the land.

Whether or not that story is authentic, we are certain that later, at the time when folksongs began to spread through Continental Europe, music was highly esteemed by the English, Irish and Scotch, and that the minstrels who journeyed among them fared well. We are told of a royal wedding which took place in 1290 and to which came four hundred and twenty-six minstrels. The bridegroom's gift to them was fifteen hundred pounds, an average of more than three pounds each.

The Norman conquest, by bringing together the Saxon and the French ideals of music and by setting up in England the feudal system with all its romantic glamor, did much to advance the cause of music. To this stimulus we are indebted for one of the most remarkable manuscripts of music now in existence— a composition written in England during the thirteenth century and called *Sumer Is Icumen In*. In form the composition is a *round*, like *Three Blind Mice*, which most of us have sung as children. You remember perhaps that in *Three Blind Mice* one singer starts the tune, and when he has sung alone for a few measures a second singer begins the same tune while the first one continues; then, a little later a third singer begins the tune while the first two continue. Thus three or more voices are singing the same tune but not together, each voice coming, of course, at just the right time to harmonize with the others.

Taken by itself the round is not a particularly important type of music except as a kind of musical exercise which has always delighted children, and often their elders as well; but it does take significance from the fact that it led to the development of *canon*, which later played an important part in some of the greatest church music that the world has ever known. Canon, in fact, is just an elaboration of the principle on which the round is based; that is, it consists of several voices singing the same tune but beginning at different times. So far as we know, *Sumer Is Icumen In* is the oldest example of music in that form.

A century or two after *Sumer Is Icumen In* was written, the condition of music in England, as well as in certain other countries, underwent an important change. The feudal system of government began to give way to more democratic forms, and with it perished the formal code of chivalry which had so favored the minstrels. These strolling musicians gradually lost their standing, until finally they were held to be little better than beggars. On the other hand, the aristocrats, the nobles, began themselves to take an interest in creating poetry and music. From the beginning of the sixteenth century, it grew fashionable for men and women of high, even noble birth, to seek distinction as musicians. King Henry VIII of England, in the early part of his reign, was especially known as a patron of music. At the coronation of his unhappy queen, Anne Boleyn, a choir of men and boys sang ballads in praise of Her Majesty.

Not many years later, by fateful chance the name of Anne Boleyn was once more connected significantly with music. But this time no choir sang her praises; she was in the Tower of London, a prisoner, writing a song on the subject of her own impending execution. The song, *O Deathe, Rock Me Asleep*, a part of which is given below, proclaims her desire to pass beyond earthly suffering. Beside the strange circumstances under which it was written, this pathetic song has two characteristics that make it noteworthy; namely, that its accompaniment does not carry the melody, as the accompaniments of all earlier songs had done, and that near the end of the composition, the melody was used to imitate the tolling of a bell. So far as known this was the first time that music had been made to represent anything outside of its own realm.

Note that the accompaniment as explained in the text of this chapter does not carry the melody.

O Deathe, Rock Me Asleep

ANNE BOLEYN (1507-1536)

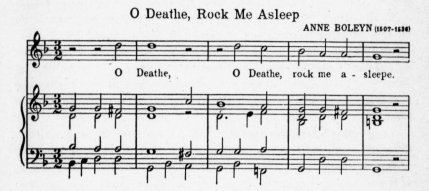

O Deathe, O Deathe, rock me a - sleepe.

The selection below taken from the end of the song, imitates the tolling of a bell.

I dye, I dye, I dye, I dye, I dye.

For about a century after the death of Anne Boleyn, the development of artistic music continued its close connection with aristocracy and the royal court. We even have surviving one or two compositions known to have come from the hand of Louis XIII of France. But about the time of Shakespeare the honors in music began to fall on men of humble birth, and the great modern era of music was commenced.

In the sixteenth century musicians began to realize the possibilities of the instruments on which they played. As they experimented they began to introduce a little variety into their music. Heretofore, in their songs, they had been content to repeat one melody over and over to each verse, but now in the development of instrumental music, some more advanced composers introduced a *second* melody, thus dividing the composition into two distinct parts. This we call the *two-part song form.*

This form was popular for many years, and it became the custom to write a succession of pieces of the song and dance type, all in one key, based on this form. These groups of pieces were called *suites* and consisted of six or eight pieces. Originally they were written for the violin, but in the seventeenth and eighteenth centuries keyboard instruments having been greatly improved, there were suites for clavichord, spinet and harpsichord. Below are examples from the *Gavotte* from Bach's *Suite in E*, which, although composed much later, is useful for illustrating the two-part song form.

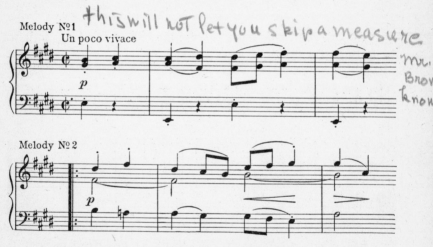

The next step was to repeat the first melody at the end of the second, thus adding a third part to the piece and forming what we call the *three-part song-form.* So, we have melody No. 1, No. 2, basis for most of our musical compositions. It is padded and enlarged in the development of sonatas and symphonies, but often and again No. 1. This simple three-part song form is the common we find it used in a very simple way, as, for example, in the following illustration from Debussy's *Reverie.*

So it was that the folk-songs of the middle ages laid the foundation for the vast structure of the music of today.

In the next chapter we shall find out how, during the period we have just studied, music developed within the Christian Church.

ORCHESTRA OF THE ELEVENTH CENTURY

The following phonograph records may be used to illustrate some of the musical selections in this chapter.

Title	Victor Record No.
THE LONDONDERRY AIR (Old Irish) (Grainger)—Philadelphia String Simfonietta.	4186
O NO, JOHN—Dadmun.	4023
SELLENGER'S ROUND—Mayfair Band.	20445
MESSIAH—AND THE GLORY OF THE LORD (Handel)—Royal Choral Society.	9125
MINNELIED—McCormack.	1272
PAVANE AND GALLIARD (William Byrd).	7873
THE CAT'S FUGUE (Domenico Scarlatti) (Harpsichord solo).	1664
BANCHETTO MUSICALE — Suite No. 1 (Schein) — Galliard — Courante—Allemande—Tripla Viole d'amour, Quinton, Viole de gamba, Viole de basse (Harpsichord).	24792

QUESTIONS

1. Tell how folksongs were created. How were they carried from town to town and from country to country during the Middle Ages?

2. Mention at least three kinds of subject which these folksongs commonly treated.

3. When and how did the practice of writing down music first become general in Europe? Was our present system of writing musical notes used from the first?

4. Who were the Troubadours? Tell what you can of their influence on the development of music.

5. Who were the Mastersingers? Can you name any other group of traveling musicians in Germany? In England?

6. What is a round? Name one. Why was the round important in the general development of music?

7. Describe fully the development of *form* in music.

Chapter IV

CHURCH MUSIC

While the folksong was taking root among the peoples of Europe and later, while the strolling players entertained medieval court and village, music was following a distinct line of growth within the Christian Church. In general, as might be supposed, this religious music had a good deal in common with secular, or non-religious music; yet so many special influences acted upon the former that its history deserves to be made a separate study. The great difference between the two types of music was primarily a difference in purpose.

Secular music, we know, had for its chief end the expression of those activities and emotions, good and bad, which made up the life of the people; church music on the contrary was expected to interpret only the nobler, more spiritual phases of that life. That distinction appears, perhaps, to be obvious; but it proved often a difficult one to maintain. From time to time secular music of no very exalted kind found its way into religious service, to such an extent that the musical history of the church, from the beginning of the Christian Era to about the end of the sixteenth century, was an almost constant swinging of the pendulum between what was noble and dignified and what was more popular but less worshipful.

In the beginning the Church had no special music of its own. Appropriate words, set to popular melodies, comprised all that existed in the way of Christian hymns. And in form, those hymns were simple, not very different from the ones in our modern hymnals. When we remember the savage persecutions that made it necessary for the Christian fathers at Rome to worship in the catacombs, unheard except by their own number, we may suppose that a good many of the songs had for their theme courage and fortitude in the face of danger. The very perils under which Christianity was practised thus served to give the early hymns a certain dignity.

It was not until the middle of the fourth century that persecution of Christians ceased. Then very rapidly the stern character of church music relaxed. Still without a special body of music composed for their own use, the Christians continued to adopt popular tunes, but not always with regard to solemnity and religious fitness. When St. Ambrose became Bishop of Milan, toward the end of the fourth century, he found much to criticize in the hymns of his church. His first step was to approve certain melodies which he thought good; then to exclude from worship tunes which were unsuited to the church service. His reforms did not consist wholly of criticism, however, for he also composed a number of new hymns, of which the most famous is that noble song of praise, *Te Deum Laudamus*. In this way he gave to the church the first great music which it could call exclusively its own.

St. Ambrose chose and composed melodies that would not only be consistent with the spirit of the hymns, but that would be pleasing to the congregation. In this action of his we have a characteristic representation of the influence of the church. Upon the aesthetic and ethical sides the church has awakened aspirations, hopes and faith of essentially musical character, and in this respect it has been one of the most powerful sources of inspiration that musical art has experienced.

Certain traces of St. Ambrose's influence have persisted, but much that he did was disrupted, when, shortly after his death, Germanic tribes from the North swept down upon Italy and conquered Rome. Had their conquest been simply one of destruction, had they sacked Italy and returned with their plunder again to the northward, the church and its music might not have undergone much permanent change. But the invaders,

ST. AMBROSE (340-397)

having conquered, settled down in Roman territory and presently took over its government. Already partly Christianized at least, they treated the church with respect and entered readily into its life. And by so doing—by introducing into the Christian congregation a new and vigorous element—they influenced church development more profoundly than they could ever have done by the torch and the sword. On the whole, Christianity was benefited by the Germanic conquest, but in the field of church music the immediate result was to undo in part the reforms of St. Ambrose. Secular music, often adapted from coarse, uncouth songs, again began to make its way into religious ceremony.

For a century or more this tendency had persisted when, in the year 590, Gregory was elected Pope. One of the first tasks he set himself was to re-organize and purify religious music. As St. Ambrose had done, he collected the best of the existing hymns and added to that body of music by composing new hymns and anthems to be sung on special days of the year. He also founded in Rome a school of singing, in which his ideals were communicated to a great number of students. In this way he introduced into the development of religious music the element of specialized training. It is chiefly because of his influence in this direction that the "plainsong" of the Roman Church and of the English Church is even to this day called Gregorian.

So thoroughgoing and sound were the Gregorian reforms that it was nearly a thousand years before the church again found necessary the revision of its music. In the meantime, during the early part of the fifteenth century, new elements were introduced into music by the so-called Netherlands school of composers. The tendency of this school, whose members became the music teachers of all Europe, was at first in the direction of difficulty and complexity. The field of music became an exercise ground for technical cleverness, with the natural result that church music again began to suffer from lack of dignity and the true spirit of devotion.

Another fault of the Netherlands school, from a church viewpoint, was that its composers, while remarkably ingenious in the rearrangement of old tunes, seemed indisposed to do anything toward the creation of tunes that were new. Consequently Christian worship was again invaded by secular tunes, thinly disguised under new and intricate musical embellishments. But even in their new form the old tunes were clearly recognizable, to such an extent that masses were frequently named after the borrowed tunes on which they were based. One, for instance, was known as the *"Adieu, My Love," Mass;* and another was called the *Mass of the Armed Man,* because its theme was taken from the following popular melody, *The Armed Man.*

The Armed Man

Fifteenth Century

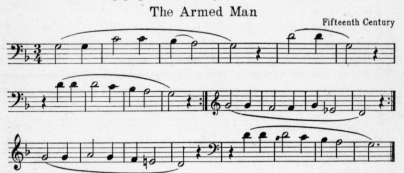

Another instance of a popular tune used for religious music is demonstrated in the following selections.

During the latter part of the sixteenth century the folksong given below, *Mein G'müth ist mir verwirret,* became widely popular:

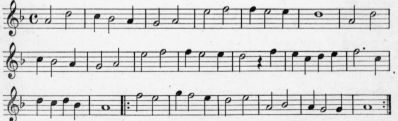

Later we find the same melody adapted, with but few changes, for use in the church service. In this use it went under the title, *O Haupt voll Blut und Wunden:*

Still other versions of the same melody appear frequently in music of a later period. A few examples are given on this and the following page.

German Love Song

Harmonized by Hasler, 1601

German Chorale

Harmonized by SCHEIN, 1627

Chorale
From "The Death of Jesus"—1755

J. G. GRAUN (1698-1771)

Chorale
From the St. Matthew Passion Music

J. S. BACH

Chorale
From J. G. Schicht's "Choralbuch"—1820

Gradually a reaction against complexity set in, and the Netherlands school began to give its attention to less intricate forms, but not until the church had absorbed a good deal of music in the earlier, involved style.

The school of the Netherlands led, in the latter part of the century, to the old Italian school, of which the shining light was

Giovanni Palestrina. Born about 1526, he composed before his death in 1594 more than ninety-five masses. His style was a fine development of the principle of *canon*, which we have already mentioned in connection with the old English tune *Sumer Is Icumen In*. Although in many respects Palestrina showed a grasp of music more perfect than that of the Netherlands school, his compositions were in effect much simpler than theirs. And while other composers were anticipating the more passionate style of the seventeenth and later centuries, Palestrina's music was still medieval in spirit, still reminiscent of monastic revery and contemplation.

Excellent in form and genuinely religious in spirit, Palestrina's work performed one great service for religious music as a whole. Under the influence of the earlier Netherlands composers, the songs of the church had at last become so artificial and sophisticated as to belie the true purpose of worship music. Numerous complaints against this tendency resulted finally in the Council of Trent, where it was debated whether or not music should be excluded from sacred service. Before the Council appeared a number of prominent composers, bringing with them works by which they

PALESTRINA (1526-1594)

hoped to prove that music was not only a suitable, but an indispensable feature of Christian worship. Of all these works, it was the *Mass of Pope Marcellus*, by Palestrina, which proved the convincing argument. Consequently, from that time on, the music of the church became more and more simple and worshipful, according to the ideal which Palestrina had set for himself;

O Bone Jesu

G. P. PALESTRINA (1526-1594)

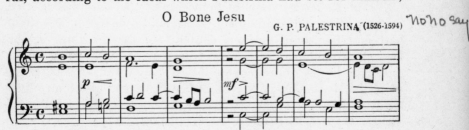

and even today his works still compose an important part of the finest music that the church calls its own. The preceding selection is an example of his style.

At the time of Palestrina the course of musical development was strongly affected by that movement in church history which gave rise to Protestantism. Martin Luther, a central figure of that movement, himself exerted a strong personal influence on music.

It was one of his principles that the congregation should take an active part in the church service and that worship should be conducted in the language of the people rather than in Latin. To that end he selected as hymn tunes melodies from the best existing folksongs, or in some cases, melodies newly composed for use as hymns. This type of music was called the *Chorale*, and was sung during church service by the congregation.

Both in Germany and in France, music not only was affected by the growth of Protestantism, but actually played an important part in establishing the new church; for the teachings of the leading Protestants were spread largely through being sung, especially by the Mastersingers in Germany. Hans Sachs, greatest of the Mastersingers, was an ardent Protestant who contributed freely to the music of the new creed. A fine example of his work, *Awake, My Heart's Beloved,* is given below:

Awake, My Heart's Beloved

HANS SACHS (1494-1576)

A - wake, my heart's be - lov - ed, Thou

Chris - tian Church, most dear, ___

etc.

The song ends with an announcement of God's goodness ("love to us aboundeth"), a thought which is carried out in the rich joyousness of the music throughout and in the following ending:

love   to   us   a -

bound - - - - eth.

Toward the middle of the sixteenth century John Calvin, a strong leader in the Protestant movement, established in Geneva a school for the purpose of training the young to sing and to qualify as teachers of music in the church. Directly, then, Calvin seemed to encourage the growth of religious music, but indirectly he exerted against music a decidedly repressive influence. His religious principles were very severe; he believed in extreme solemnity and simplicity of worship. In his congregation at Geneva no music was approved except metrical versions of the Psalms set to music. One such musical Psalm, written by Louis Bourgeois, a close friend of Calvin, has survived to this day in the Doxology, *Praise God From Whom All Blessings Flow.* But many of the other hymns similarly composed lacked the fine spirit of the Doxology, and on the whole Calvin's followers had a rather dreary body of music.

The same general tendencies which characterized Calvin and his group later developed into that phase of Protestant reaction which we call Puritanism. Devout and dignified in their interpretation of moral laws, the Puritans were too austere to develop or even approve any but the most formal music. When under Oliver Cromwell Puritanism attained its greatest power in government, all ceremony in church worship and consequently most church music, suffered the most violent attacks and denunciation. Vestments were abolished, choirs were disbanded, and almost every organ in England was destroyed.

When the Puritans came to America, they brought with them their Psalm-tunes and their hatred of secular music. But in their new homes, with all the cares that descended on them, the early colonists found no time even to keep their knowledge of music, scant as it was. Many of the Psalm-tunes sung by the Pilgrim Fathers sank presently into oblivion; and it is said that for a period of eighty or ninety years not more than ten different tunes, if so many, were used in public worship.

But while the influence of Puritanism tended to discourage progress in music, the influence of this period of religious discussion as a whole proved genuinely stimulating to most of the arts, music included. In the field of intellect old ideals were readjusted, new problems were brought up, fresh consideration was given to principles so old that they were almost forgotten; and in the field of art new technique was developed, freer expression was given to the emotions, and a new era of song was begun. Within less than a century after Luther first broke away from the Roman Church, the whole atmosphere of the Middle Ages had given way to a spirit more modern and more nearly like the spirit of our own times.

How church music responded to its new setting, especially under the guidance of Bach and Handel, we shall discuss in the next chapter.

The following phonograph records may be used to illustrate some of the musical selections in this chapter.

Title	Victor Record No.
POPULE MEUS (Palestrina).	20898
VENI CREATOR SPIRITUS (Ambrosian Chant).	20896
MAGNIFICAT (Gregorian Chant) Palestrina Choir.	20897
HYMN IN HONOR OF SAINT JOHN—Palestrina Choir.	20897
MISSA PAPAE MARCELLI (Mass—Pope Marcellus)—	
(Palestrina) Westminster Cathedral Choir.	35941-35944
GREGORIAN CHANTS.	24819-24820

QUESTIONS

1. Explain briefly the difference in purpose between religious and secular (non-religious) music.
2. What sort of themes were used for hymns up to the time of St. Ambrose?
3. Who was St. Ambrose? What was the character of his reforms?
4. Compare the Gregorian music with that of the Netherlands school of composers.
5. What were the characteristics of Palestrina's music? How was Palestrina connected with the Council of Trent?
6. What effect did Martin Luther and his followers have upon church music?

Chapter V

BACH AND HANDEL

During the Middle Ages progress in the art of music, like progress in most of the other arts, was gradual. In any one century few musicians became important enough to attract attention, and musical theory remained unchanged and unimproved from generation to generation. Considering how tedious were the means of travel in those days, how few were the libraries and how scant the facilities for spreading knowledge, it is not at all remarkable that musical development should have been sluggish.

But from about the first of the sixteenth century the circulation of knowledge, and consequently the development of the arts became more and more rapid. The invention of the printing-press, the increasing ease of travel from place to place, the vast improvement in education—all tended to quicken progress. Through the sixteenth and seventeenth centuries we see music making rapid gains in new principles and refinements; but it is in the eighteenth century that music really falls into a steady stride. From that time on we shall find our musical history packed with important names and significant events. To the development of music in the first part of the eighteenth century we shall devote the present chapter.

The year 1685 gave to the world two names that are often linked in musical history—Bach and Handel. The lives of these men in a number of external respects were remarkably similar. Both were born in the same year; both were Germans; both composed great religious works; both were masterly organists; and both in their later years were stricken blind. But as we study the works of each, we shall find that the music of Bach and the music of Handel were decidedly unlike.

From very childhood, Johann Sebastian Bach recognized in music the great purpose of his life. He came of a large family which had long been prominent musically and which was noted for its simple virtue, piety, and thrift. His family belonged to the peasant class, and its musical activity was pursued in connection with churches and town bands.

46

To gain the musical education he wanted, Bach was obliged to undergo many hardships. After the death of his parents he went to live with his older brother, Johann Christoph, an organist, who for some reason undertook to discourage the younger Bach from the study of music. The story is told that Johann Christoph possessed a number of interesting manuscripts which Bach was eager to study, but the brother refused to let him examine them. Not to be denied Bach though only a boy, made it a practice to creep downstairs after the family had gone to bed, take the music up to his room, and there by moonlight painstakingly copy it. The strain that this custom put upon his eyes probably led to the blindness which afflicted him years afterward.

The same earnestness of purpose which led Bach as a boy to copy music at midnight made it possible for him eventually to master the art of composition. Taking the works of earlier composers, he studied them minutely and strove always to improve on them. But the end he had in view was not merely to win credit for his own ability as a musician. Strongly attached to the principles of Martin Luther, he made it his conscious aim to build up for the Evangelical Church a worthy body of music. His secular works, numerous and valuable as they are, he considered merely as a diversion from his absorbing interest in religious music. Much the larger portion of Bach's works consist of vocal compositions for the church—cantatas, passions, and the like. Among the most famous of his works is the *Passion according to St. Matthew*, a touching portrayal in music of the feeling of a devout believer who contemplates the suffering and death of Christ.

The Italian music of Bach's time, and for that matter of later periods, was dominated by a passion for pure melody. Bach closely studied that Italian style and appreciated it; yet his own work showed usually characteristics of a stronger, sturdier kind, which were in reality a reflection of his Teutonic life. He sought a richer, deeper expression than any that could be gained by the conventional Italian treatment of melody with simple accompaniment. His chords were full and robust, his rhythms, especially in the music which he wrote for the dances of that period, were clean-cut and strong. Even so brief an example

JOHANN SEBASTIAN BACH (1685-1750)

as the *Bourrée* quoted below will serve to indicate how broad and wholesome was Bach's musical feeling.

Bourrée

From the Second Violin Sonata

Yet on occasions he was capable of creating music which for melodic sweetness was unsurpassed by the best masters of Italy. And indeed his *Air* given here combines in fine proportion the melody of the Italian school with the sturdiness of the German ideal.

On the practical—one might say mechanical—side of music, Bach made one contribution of the greatest importance. Previously the clavichord, an ancestor of the piano, had been tuned in such a way that modulation, or changing from one key to

Air from the Suite in D

J. S BACH 1685-1750

another in the course of a composition, resulted in tone combinations that were almost discords. Bach, foreseeing that such a limitation on the part of the instrument must inevitably hinder any broad development in clavichord music, worked out a system of "equal temperament" so-called, which made possible easy and musical modulations. With his own instrument tuned according to that system, he then composed a series of preludes and fugues which he called *The Well-tempered Clavichord.*

While the original purpose of this collection was to prove the soundness of the "equal temperament" idea, the various compositions which it includes have always been recognized as remarkable examples of technical skill. The fugues in particular show his mastery of counterpoint; that is, the weaving together of several themes or tunes. In one fugue, for example, we find this theme at the beginning.

Fugue V
From "The Well-Tempered Clavichord" Vol. I
J. S. BACH

Presently the counter theme B is introduced.

And later we find both themes brought closely together, as though one were a question and the other its answer.

A summary of Bach's achievements proves him to have been a composer of deep religious feeling, a master of the broad, rich Teutonic style, a practical inventor of musical method, and a skilled workman in the intricate technique of his day.

The music of Handel in many ways differs from that of Bach. Though himself a German, Handel followed very closely the musical ideal of the Italians. Like them he sought to produce melody supported by only a slight accompaniment. The more solid harmonies so characteristic of Bach, Handel took no pains to develop, though his Teutonic feeling led him to create a rather richer type of melody than was usual with Italian composers.

HANDEL (1685-1759)

It was natural that, with his leaning toward pure tunefulness, Handel's greatest achievement should be in the field of the human voice—of song. His instrumental compositions all reveal skillful workmanship, but comparatively they are of minor importance. The bulk of his work falls into two classes: operas and oratorios. To both these forms he was attached not alone by the fact that his music was appropriate to them but also by the fact that he was for some time manager of an opera house in London. His close contact with musical audiences made it possible for him to create works of wide popularity.

His operas, however, though they were well received at the period when they were written, have not well survived the test of time. Perhaps they were adjusted too exactly to the tastes of the eighteenth century—a taste which has since been greatly modified. Separate airs such as the *Largo* from *Xerxes*, are still enjoyed, but his operas as a whole have vanished from the stage.

Handel's clearest title to greatness lies in his oratorios. Before his time that form of music had attained no high development. In the year 1561, St. Philip Neri, having founded a congregation of the clergy at Rome, had introduced for its instruction and enjoyment the rendering of sacred plays set to music. The words of these plays were taken from versified arrangements of Bible stories; the music consisted of four-part choruses, varied by occasional solo passages. And because they were performed in the vestibule, or oratory, of the chapel the plays were called "oratorios." During the century and a half that passed before Handel's day, other composers took over and developed the oratorio form, but little of their work was destined to last.

Handel himself was first attracted to the oratorio form not

Air—He Shall Feed His Flock Like a Shepherd

Larghetto, e piano

G. F. HANDEL (1685-1759)

as a composer, but as a business manager. In charge of a London opera house, he faced each year a dull period during the Lenten season, when no operas were produced. Principally to keep the opera house open, he introduced the oratorio as a type of performance appropriate to religious observance. He made no attempt in the beginning to create new works for his audiences, but contented himself with patching together fragments of earlier productions. The experiment was successful, and in 1740 he began to devote most of his attention to composing oratorios. From that point dates his period of greatest achievement. Many of his airs remain to this day unsurpassed in religious music for beauty and pathos.

If we make a careful study of Handel's whole career, we cannot help feeling too that while he developed the oratorio, the oratorio also developed and brought out the finest musical instincts in him. Whereas some of his earlier work is merely skillful, his oratorios show a genuinely deep sense of religion, a fine grasp of the spirit as well as the technique of his whole subject. We need examine only the Pastoral from his *Messiah* just quoted to appreciate the honesty and depth of his feeling.

This pastoral, we are told, owes its origin to a group of Italian peasants, the *Pifferari* who according to ancient custom appeared in Rome about Christmas of each year to perform their pastoral melodies before the shrines of the Holy Virgin. Thus, Handel made use of folk music, and in adapting it he destroyed not a bit of the noble folk spirit.

Because he was so earnestly in sympathy with his subject, Handel was able in one important respect to improve on the Italian style which had served him as a model. The typical Italian composers had not troubled themselves greatly to give their music the shading which we call "expression"; indeed the light character of their melodies, the absence of feeling, had made expression a conventional, superficial affair to be added according to the taste of the singer. But the religious melodies of Handel's oratorios were so filled with spiritual emotion that the most unimaginative singer could not fail to give them appropriate expression. And therein lies, perhaps, the strongest evidence of Handel's genius: that in his best works the expression is an unmistakable, inseparable part of his music.

Handel died in 1759 leaving to the world, beside operas and minor works, more than twenty oratorios. Bach had died nine years earlier. But already the new generation was taking its place, ready to build on the foundation, both in melody and in harmony, which Handel and Bach had laid. In the next chapter we shall trace the development of that newer school through the works of its two principal figures—Haydn and Mozart.

The following phonograph records may be used to illustrate some of the musical selections in this chapter.

Title   Victor
                                                           Record No.

LARGO FROM *Xerxes* (Handel)—Chicago Symphony Orchestra.   6648

Title	Victor Record No.
HE SHALL FEED HIS FLOCK (from *Messiah*) (Handel)— Matzenauer.	6555
PASTORAL SYMPHONY (from *Messiah*) (Handel)—Victor Concert Orchestra.	20620
MENUET NOS. 1 AND 2 (Bach)—Kreisler.	1136
TOCCATA AND FUGUE (Bach)—Philadelphia Symphony.	6751
MASS IN B MINOR (Bach) Famous Artists, Choir, London Symphony.	9955-9971
HALLELUJAH CHORUS—*Messiah* (Handel)—Trinity Choir.	35768
PASTORAL SYMPHONY (*Christmas Oratorio*); CHORALE (*Within yon gloomy manger*); MARCH IN D MAJOR; COME, LET US TO THE BAGPIPE'S SOUND (*Peasant's Cantata*); (Bach)—Victor Orchestra.	24793

QUESTIONS

1. Name two celebrated musicians who were born in the year 1685. Mention several respects in which their lives appear remarkably similar.

2. Tell briefly of some of the hardships that Bach was obliged to undergo in order to obtain his musical education. In what sort of music was he most interested?

3. For what particular purpose did he compose the series of fugues called *The Well-tempered Clavichord?*

4. In what general ways did Handel's music differ from that of Bach? What forms of composition include Handel's greatest masterpieces?

5. Give the origin of the "oratorio." State briefly the circumstances which led to Handel's unexcelled achievements in this particular form of music.

Chapter VI

HAYDN AND MOZART

This chapter deals with the music of the classical period. It must be kept in mind just what distinguishes the music of that period, if the contrast between it and the ensuing period is to be appreciated. The composers of the classical period strove for beauty of line, of form; they chiseled their music from harmonic material as a sculptor chisels from marble. Foremost of all, their music was based on intellectual principles and was not made to express any particular emotions. In this, classical composers differed from those who followed them.

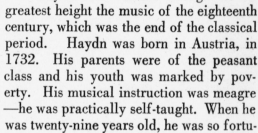

HAYDN

Haydn and Mozart brought to its greatest height the music of the eighteenth century, which was the end of the classical period. Haydn was born in Austria, in 1732. His parents were of the peasant class and his youth was marked by poverty. His musical instruction was meagre —he was practically self-taught. When he was twenty-nine years old, he was so fortunate as to be taken into the service of the Esterhazy family which was very powerful and rich. He remained under its support throughout his life.

The relations of Haydn to this family suggest one of the most interesting phases of the musical life of the time. Before the establishment of the public concert system and musical publishing business of the present day, musicians derived their subsistance from the patronage of the aristocracy. Titled and wealthy families maintained private musical establishments, monopolizing the services of composers and performers. The social position of the latter was hardly above that of the house-servants. This patronage of the nobility was considered necessary to the progress of secular music in the seventeenth and eighteenth centuries. But as composition of instrumental music progressed, public concerts were regarded more favorably. As long as the artists were mostly singers their performances were, to a great extent, dependent upon the co-operation of others. Instrumental music needed no support for it furnished its own harmonic background. Therefore performers began to be recognized for their individual merits and they were encouraged to improve their art. The gradual growth of the custom of giving public concerts contributed much to the development of the composition of instrumental music.

Haydn was a musician of great foresight and prophetic power. Therein lies his greatest importance in musical history. His compositions reveal conspicuously the universal tendency to write music for social and domestic entertainment. For a long time the best composers had devoted their talent to the improvement of the music in the church and to the expression of religious feeling; but now a desire was arising to write music for the home and for more popular enjoyment.

Haydn, being a peasant, was familiar with the music of his class. He keenly enjoyed and sympathized with their village bands and out-door musical gatherings. The bright, cheerful spirit of their dance-music is breathed in the elasticity of Haydn's rhythms and the brightness of his melody. An example of Haydn's work, *Andante with Variations,* is given below:

Theme of the Variations in F minor

F. J. HAYDN (1732-1809)

The love of music, the talent for it among the unlearned folk have always had far-reaching influences. Their melodies and their dance rhythms have formed the basis for the compositions of the learned composers. But in the eighteenth century the musical activities of the common people also affected the growth of music by developing the principles of instrumental composition. Before the time of Haydn there were only two branches in which first-rate and mature instrumental work had been done. There were compositions for the violin and clavier. Haydn saw clearly the new capacities of instrumental music and pointed the way to their fulfillment by later masters. He made use of instruments for solo work which had never before been so used. In doing this he improved the sonata form. A sonata is an instrumental composition, usually of three or four distinct movements, each complete, yet all related so as to form a perfect whole. This type of composition is used for the piano only, or piano and another instrument. A form similar to that of the sonata is also applied to symphonies and string quartets. Haydn first established the classical sonata form and the principles which are now the basis of good quartet writing.

The *sonata form* is an enlargement, greatly padded, of that simple structure in three parts described in the first and third chapters. There we had a main theme (A), a contrasting theme (B), and again the main theme (A). In the sonata-form the three parts do not content themselves with only one theme apiece. We still have the *main* theme but it has a contrasting theme all its own and these two make the first part, *A*. The second part, *B*, instead of an entirely different theme, develops and presents from different angles portions of the themes which make *A*. The third part, again *A*, brings back the first part with triumphant emphasis on the main theme. This is the skeleton of the sonata-form:

A	B	A
EXPOSITION	DEVELOPMENT	RECAPITULATION
1. Main theme. 2. Contrasting theme.	Working up of material given.	Return of main theme in original form. Contrasting theme.

At least one movement of a sonata must be written according to this form. A *symphony* is a sonata written for full orchestra.

Another great improvement Haydn made was in the treatment of the instruments of the orchestra. Haydn, seeing the possibilities of other instruments than the violin for solo use, established the essential principles of orchestration, and those principles survive to the present day. The stringed instruments usually sustain the chief melody, and the wood-wind and brass are used to develop and enrich the general effect. Any instrument, however, may at times lead in the melody, the themes being passed from one to another. Modern orchestration dates from Haydn.

The reform Haydn began was completed by Mozart. He was born in 1756, the child of a professional musician. He was extraordinarily precocious on the piano and violin, and at the age of six he made a concert tour. His first published compositions belong to 1763—when he was only seven. His first opera was written when he was twelve. At the age of thirteen he visited Italy and there became acquainted with Italian opera.

MOZART AT 14

When he was twenty-five Mozart took up his permanent abode in Vienna. Here began a time of bitter struggle which ended only with his death. Although a composer at that period was dependent upon patronage, Mozart never obtained a permanent situation, and lucrative commissions were rare. Poverty and hardship wore out his strength and he was buried in a pauper's grave when only thirty-five.

Mozart worked in every field of music known to his time. His works are often cited as the most perfect illustrations of the classical idea in music. This term, remember, refers to the absence of *individualism*, and conformity to a *general type* of style and form. Abstract, objective beauty is the aim rather than the license that results from arbitrary self-expression.

Mozart is the most complete illustration in music history of the sensitive, spontaneous musical temperament. To an unsurpassed musical instinct, he added a supreme mastery of the musical science of his day. To Italian melody, limpid and flowing, he gave a substructure of Teutonic learning and seriousness, although the more obvious qualities of his art are Italian rather than German. He gave the final stamp of elegance and restrained dignity to eighteenth century musical art and completed the epoch that preceded the revolutionary attacks of Beethoven and his successors. *The Violet* quoted below is a typical example of his style.

The Violet

W. A. MOZART (1756-1791)

Mozart further improved the sonata form. In his last three symphonies he displayed a feeling for individuality of style. He wrote them all in one year and they are known as the symphonies in E flat, A minor, and C major. His concertos for piano and orchestra take a high place; but it was in his symphonies that he advanced the art of orchestration, for they surpassed Haydn's in freedom of the use of the instruments, as well as in depth of expression and power of development.

Not only did Mozart understand the simplicity of the Italian melody, and the dramatic seriousness of German harmony, but he also absorbed French rhythm. France had already begun to strive for reality in music. Her composers sought to portray nature and reality instead of achieving abstract beauty. They had developed a faculty for graceful rhythm. By combining German depth, Italian melody, and French rhythm, Mozart first raised music to the point where it could make an international appeal.

His most important and original contribution to musical art was in his later operas: *The Marriage of Figaro, Don Giovanni* and *The Magic Flute.* These are the most important works of their class in the eighteenth century, and they mark the highest achievement of Italian song as applied to dramatic purposes. In the importance which they give to poetic truth and natural action they reveal how earnestly Mozart studied the French school.

Mozart's last opera, *The Magic Flute,* is less valuable musically than *Figaro* and *Don Giovanni,* but it has great historic interest from the fact that its text is German, and its subject and treatment foreshadow the nineteenth century school of German romantic opera.

It was in *The Magic Flute,* too, that the influence of the German *Lied,* or folksong, first became apparent in artistic and highly developed music. Earlier composers had rather looked down upon the *Lied* because of its humble origin. But now Mozart recognized it as being worthy of recognition in opera. In the century following, Schubert recognized the excellence of the German *Lied* and devoted much of his life to winning for it the general appreciation it deserved.

The following phonograph records may be used to illustrate some of the musical selections in this chapter.

Title	Victor Record No.
SERENADE (*Eine Kleine Nachtmusik*) (Mozart)—Chamber Orchestra.	9789-9790
VOI CHE SAPETE (from *The Marriage of Figaro*) (Mozart)— Elisabeth Schumann.	7076
BATTI, BATTI, O BEL MASETTO (from *Don Giovanni*) (Mozart) Elisabeth Schumann.	7076
SYMPHONY, No. 2 (*London*) (Haydn) Barbirolli's Orchestra.	35981-35983
SYMPHONY IN C MAJOR (*Jupiter*) (Mozart) Coates and London Symphony Orchestra.	9201-9204
SURPRISE SYMPHONY NO. 6 (Haydn).	M-55

Title	Victor Record No.
QUARTET IN D MAJOR (Haydn)—Elman String Quartet.	6701-6702
MAGIC FLUTE—Chorus of Priests—Metropolitan Opera Chorus.	4027
MAGIC FLUTE—Overture (Mozart)—Philharmonic Orchestra.	1486
ADAGIO IN D MAJOR AND ANDANTE (FINALE) (from *Clock Symphony*)—Haydn.	24794

QUESTIONS

1. What were the outstanding characteristics of music of the classical period?

2. Tell what you can of Haydn's influence on eighteenth century music.

3. What is the sonata form? In what way did Haydn improve this form of music?

4. What are the underlying principles of orchestration? How do present-day methods compare with those established by Haydn?

5. Describe as definitely as you can the qualities of Mozart's music. How was his style influenced by the music of other nations than his own?

6. What effect did the growing custom of giving public concerts in the latter part of the eighteenth century have on music?

Chapter VII

OPERA

In the chapter on *Songs of the Middle Ages* we learned that a step towards operatic composition was made in the thirteenth century by Adam de la Halle when he wrote his *Le Jeu de Robert et Marion*. A second effort in this direction was not made until the sixteenth century. A group of Florentine gentlemen were in the habit of meeting at the palace of one of their members for the purpose of studying Greek literature. They were inspired to attempt a reproduction of Greek art with the aid of music. What is considered by some historians as the first opera was the result of their efforts. This was *Dafne*, composed by Peri and Caccini, with text by Rinnucini, in 1597. The *recitative* —a form of *musical declamation*—was applied for the first time to a whole play in Dafne.

Three years later (1600) Peri produced publicly in Florence his opera *Euridice*, based on the popular Greek story of Orpheus. An example from it is given here.

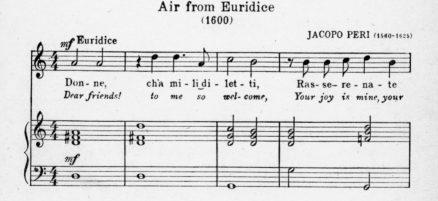

Air from Euridice
(1600)

JACOPO PERI (1560-1625)

Don- ne, ch'a mi - li di - let - ti, Ras- se- re - na - te
Dear friends! *to* *me* *so* *wel- come,* *Your joy is mine, your*

si lo sguar-do e'l vol - to, Che den-tre a' vos-tri pet - ti
glad-ness mine in - creas - es, And nought with-in your bo   som

Tut - to ras - sem-bra il mio gio - ir   rac - col -
But finds an an - swer in mine own con - tent - -

to.   Deh____ co - me lie - ta as - col - to i dol - ci
ment.   Oh!____ how my soul is stirred by your sweet

can - ti,   E gl'a - mo - ro   si det - ti d'a -
greet - ings Your ten - der words and prais - es of

mor, Di cor-te-sia gra-di - - ti af-fet - ti.
love, *Your gen-tle acts of kind___ af-fec - tion.*

Caccini (1546-1615) also made a setting of this poem. For the marriage of Henry IV and Maria de' Medici at Florence in 1600 a version made up of both arrangements was performed. Peri's version opens with a prologue in recitative style, with *ritornelli*—little passages which recur frequently like a refrain. The dialogue continues in recitative, with here and there a chorus interjected. There is a free chord accompaniment. Caccini's version is in the same style except that he gives the voice parts more florid treatment. The use of the simple accompaniment, and the new freedom given the voice, mark the beginning of a new era in the history of music.

The joint production of Peri's and Caccini's settings of *Euridice* mark the beginning of real musical drama. The preceding efforts in that direction had more resembled oratorio than drama. Even *Euridice* illustrates the combination of the Mystery with stories of classical mythology. But it was an eminent musician of Venice, Claudio Monteverde (1568-1643), who found courage to break away from the timid and restrained recitative and lead his solo to the stage of the *arioso*, which is an abbreviated form of the aria; that is, a melody sung as a solo. Monteverde experimented with the use of instruments, endeavoring to achieve combinations which would intensify sentiment and situation. His efforts aroused the enthusiasm of the whole musical world. Other composers became ambitious to imitate Monteverde and to improve on him. This interest in opera led to the establishment in Venice of the first opera house in 1637.

It was Cavalli (1600-1676), a pupil of Monteverde, who gave full recognition to the *aria* as distinct from the recitative.

He appreciated the value of a lyrical passage through solo song in every strong dramatic situation.

Allessandro Scarlatti (1659-1725), the greatest Italian composer of the seventeenth century, gave more symmetry to the aria, elaborated the recitative and with his contrapuntal mastery enriched the orchestration and led the way in making the overture more independent.

CONCERT BY SCARLATTI, TARTINI, MARTINI, LOCATELLI AND LANZETTI

Cavalli had a great influence over Lully (1633-1687), an Italian who went to France and was granted a monopoly of opera production by Louis XV in 1672. He became almost the sole composer of opera for France until his death in 1687. Lully was a better dramatist and stage manager than musician. In spite of a considerable gift for melody, his operas were pompous and stiff. He did not, however, rely solely on poetry and music for his effects, but endeavored to enhance the dramatic situations by stage-settings, pantomime, and dancing. In this respect he differed from the Italians who permitted musical effect to be all important. Lully sought for union between poetry, music and action.

However, his operas are formal and artificial. His successors did not improve upon Lully's style which prevailed in France until past the middle of the eighteenth century. The taste of the French people began to revolt against the stiffness of the opera and conditions were ripe for the reforms of a German who appeared in Paris in 1774. This was Christoph Willibald von Gluck (1714-1787).

Gluck was born near Nuremberg. At the age of twenty-two he went to Vienna to study music. He skilfully adapted himself to the standards of the operatic world as he found them. In Italy the "opera seria"—the serious or tragic opera—was popular. The seventeenth century has contributed to opera the recitative as the best means of developing active situations and the aria as the solo by which a leading character expresses intense emotion. The chorus was seldom used and was almost a part of the stage setting. Scenery and costuming were too spectacular. The characters in an opera were usually represented by three or four male and three female characters, the hero being a high tenor and the heroine a soprano. Until about the middle of the eighteenth century the latter was an artificial male soprano for women singers were not liked. Voices of low register were considered unimportant.

The interpretation of the recitative and aria was left largely to the singer. With the establishment of the aria there began a marked driftaway from the oratorio style which had been typical of the operas, toward always greater freedom of melody for the singer. At last the result was that Italian opera became like a concert program whereon individual singers displayed their skill. Composers were forced to write sensuous melody which would reveal the prowess of the performers. The dramatic side of the opera could hardly be considered.

This was the type of opera which Gluck first wrote. But he was not contented with it and he began to experiment in another direction. Gradually arose in other countries the "opera buffa," or comic opera, which scorned the conventions established by the "opera seria." The tendency in this direction paved the way for the exploitation of the theories which Gluck finally adopted. But his efforts were not greatly liked by the Italians, who still preferred the flowing melody sung by a brilliant artist.

So in 1774 Gluck went to Paris. The temperament of the French people was better attuned to the kind of opera Gluck wished to write. He was encouraged and assisted by Marie Antoinette, formerly one of his pupils. From then on Gluck developed, until he became the greatest eighteenth century exponent of dramatic music.

GLUCK

A fairly complete understanding of Gluck's ideals can be gained from his dedication to the opera *Alceste* which was produced in 1776. He wrote: "I endeavored to reduce music to its proper function, that of seconding poetry by enforcing the expression of the sentiment and the interest of the situations, without interrupting the action or weakening it by superfluous ornament." That is, he believed that the dramatic text was the most important part of the opera, and that the music should be not only beautiful by itself but also capable of interpreting the dramatic action.

I Have Lost My Euridice

CHRISTOPHER GLUCK
(1714-1787)

At another point in the same dedication he wrote: "My idea was that the overture ought to indicate the subject and prepare the spectators for the character of the piece they are about to see; that the instruments ought to be introduced in proportion to the degree of interest and passion in the words."

In that statement there is a good deal to suggest the later revolutionary reforms of Wagner; and indeed we may regard Gluck as having been no less radical, for the time in which he lived, than was Wagner at a later period.

Let us now proceed to the nineteenth century. In Italy this century produced some brilliant examples of Italian "bel canto." There were especially Rossini's *Barber of Seville*, Donizetti's *Lucia di Lammermoor*, Bellini's *La Sonnambula*, and Verdi's *Rigoletto*, *La Traviata* and *Il Trovatore*. These operas still hold the stage in the world's opera houses, because they possess genius and vitality which is superior to their outmoded form. Some of the singers who did much to make these operas famous in their day were Jenny Lind, Grisi, Malibran, Sontag, Patti, Sembrich, sopranos; Alboni and Scalchi, contraltos; Rubini, Tamberlik, Mario, Tamagno, Campanini, and Caruso, tenors; Lablache, bass. The display of such talent would always be a pleasure, but today our taste in opera is better satisfied by music that is more than merely tuneful: we want the opera to be alive —vital. To appreciate how superficial in general was the dramatic feeling in nineteenth century Italian opera, let us take the aria from *Lucia di Lammermoor*, which Lucia, insane, sings after murdering the husband she had been tricked into marrying. In this aria, which is given below, she is calling for the lover from whom she had been separated. There is but little in the music, it must be conceded, to convey insanity or impassioned longing.

Lucia di Lammermoor

bright___ dawns___ the fu-ture, with - out___ a___

cloud, smil - ing be - fore___ us, smil - ing be -

fore___ us, bright dawns the fu ture with - out a

cloud.___ Ah,___ yes,___ with-out a

This same century in France produced operas which are still played before enthusiastic audiences. Gounod's *Faust*, Bizet's *Carmen*, Massenet's *Thaïs* and Saint-Saën's *Samson et Dalila* are outstanding examples of this period. Of these *Carmen* is recognized as one of the most individual and powerful works the French stage has ever known. It is also interesting to note that Saint-Saëns, composer of *Samson et Dalila*, ranks as one of the most versatile among recent musicians, and has to his credit not only operas but various instrumental works of great beauty.

SAINT-SAËNS

Of all modern operas Gounod's *Faust* is perhaps the most popular. The Faust legend inspired Goethe's great poem which in turn inspired Gounod whose opera was first performed in Paris, March 19, 1859, and in the United States, in New York, November 25, 1863. In the third act Faust seeing Marguerite's humble dwelling voices his admiration for her innocence in the romance *Salut! demeure chaste et pure,* here given.

All Hail, Thou Dwelling Pure and Lowly
From "Faust"

CHARLES GOUNOD
(1818-1893)

En ce ré - duit, que de fé - li - ci - té!__
*Of peace and love and in-no-cence un-told!*__

It was in Germany that the most radical reformer of opera was born during the nineteenth century. Richard Wagner (1813-1883) achieved all that Gluck had visioned. His operas are the most powerful, dramatically and musically, of any ever written. Wagner was not only a composer but also a philosophic thinker.

He tried to show that dramatic art might be made the mirror of the forces that work for progress in human life and at the same time contribute to the betterment of society through its convincing presentation of the highest ideals.

WAGNER (1813-1883)

The story of the early part of Wagner's life is one of a miserable struggle with poverty and an unsympathetic public. In 1849 he was implicated, whether justly or not is not known, in an attempt at revolution in Saxony. To avoid arrest he was forced to make a precipitate flight into Switzerland, and there he endured thirteen years of exile. During this period he developed his theories of art.

Wagner wrote his own librettos. He believed that if music must be true to poetry, poetry must be true to itself, and he would trust no one but himself to prepare his texts.

As a "musical scene-painter" Wagner's supremacy is not denied. He made his orchestra an important part of the dramatic picture, and in fact gave his leading melodies to the instruments rather than to the voices. Then, having freed the voices from the necessity of carrying the air, he wove them into his general harmonic and melodic scheme.

Another innovation by which Wagner upset all the pre-conceived ideas of opera was his introduction of the *Leit-motif*, a musical theme attached to some person or idea or event in the opera. When, to take a very simple example, a certain character first makes his appearance on the stage, a particular Leit-motif appears in the music; the Leit-motif identifies the character; and whenever later in the piece the Leit-motif occurs, it is always in a certain relation with the character. Sometimes, when the action on the stage is influenced indirectly by a character, though the character himself does not appear, his Leit-motif, occurring in the music, reveals his influence. It is largely through this device that Wagner's music is able to interpret so subtly the dramatic ideas of his operas, and to reflect the slightest change of movement, mood or situation on the stage.

The opera which carries to the furthest possible completion Wagner's theories of the union of music and dramatic poetry is *Tristan and Isolde*. In this he has not endeavored to depict Tristan and Isolde as distinct personalities, but love as a quality, affected by and affecting various conditions. The most important theme is that with which the prelude to the opera begins:—

Prelude to Tristan and Isolde

RICHARD WAGNER (1813-1883)

Note that it is two-voiced and that one voice ascends thus:

while the other descends:

This theme is the symbol of the ill-fated love which Wagner depicted in his opera. The rising voice expresses longing and hope; the descending expresses despair and the knowledge that the love can never be fulfilled. Throughout the first act we find this theme recurring, for it is in this act that there is born that love which is to cause so much suffering. In the prelude to the second act we hear the rising voice by itself. When the curtain rises we find Isolde waiting for Tristan; they have planned a secret meeting. That rising voice thus indicates the increasing passion of love, forgetful for the time of its futility and hopelessness. During the dialogue between Tristan and Isolde the orchestra develops this theme.

In this duet the passion of the lovers reaches its height; they long for the life beyond death, when their love may be made perfect.

In the last act death comes to them. Beside Tristan's body Isolde expends her own last strength in singing the *Love Death*. The melody is the same which accompanied the Love-Duet of the second act. Thus Wagner uses one motif to accompany both the desire for death, and the coming of death. While dying, Isolde is again, as in the Love-Duet, conscious only of the love existing between Tristan and herself. How fitting it is that the motif which guided the lovers through their passion should guide them into that life together for which they longed!

The public was slow to recognize the beauty of Wagner's operas. It could not appreciate his idea that the music should be made subordinate to the dramatic text and still wanted the easily comprehended melodic style of the old Italian school. But public taste has since come to appreciate and acclaim his greatness. Speaking in the broadest sense, Wagner's conception of the mutual relations of music, poetry and action will probably remain henceforth the basis of all opera.

Further mention of opera will be made later in the book. Meanwhile, in the next chapter, we shall take up the transition from the Classical period to the Romantic period in music, with emphasis on the work of Beethoven.

The following phonograph records may be used to illustrate some of the musical selections in this chapter.

Title	Victor Record No.
MAD SCENE from *Lucia di Lammermoor* (Donizetti)—Pons.	7369
ANVIL CHORUS from *Il Trovatore* (Verdi)—Victor Mixed Chorus.	20127
WALTZ from *Faust* (Gounod)—Metropolitan Opera.	9697
SALUT! DEMEURE from *Faust* (Gounod)—Lauri-Volpi Chorus.	7389
MÉDITATION from *Thaïs* (Massenet)—Kreisler.	6844
DEPUIS LE JOUR from *Louise* (Charpentier)—Bori.	6561
PRELUDE TO ACT III OF *Lohengrin* (Wagner)—Philadelphia Symphony Orchestra.	6791
DIE MEISTERSINGER — Overture (Wagner) — Karl Muck and Berlin State Opera Orchestra.	6858-6859
TANNHÄUSER—Overture (Wagner)—Coates and Symphony Orchestra.	9059-9060
WILLIAM TELL—Overture (Rossini)—Victor Symphony Orchestra.	20606-20607
SAMSON ET DALILA—MON COEUR S'OUVRE À TA VOIX (Saint-Saëns) Matzenauer.	6531
SAMSON ET DALILA—BACCHANALE (Saint-Saëns)—Philadelphia Orchestra.	6823
CARMEN—Habanera (Bizet)—Jeritza.	8091
CARMEN—Toreador Song (Act II) (Bizet)—Tibbett.	8124
EURIDICE (Peri and Caccini)—Non piango—Crane.	21752
BARBER OF SEVILLE—Largo al factotum (Rossini)—Tibbett.	7353
AÏDA (Verdi) Chorus and Orchestration of La Scala, Milan.	9488-9506
ORFEO (Gluck) Che farò senza Euridice—Onegin.	6803
FAUST (Gounod)—Soldier's Chorus—Victor Male Chorus.	19783

Title	Victor Record No.
RIGOLETTO (Verdi) La Scala, Milan.	9525-9539
TRISTAN UND ISOLDE (Wagner) Prelude—San Francisco Orchestra.	6585
LIEBESTOD—Symphony Orchestra.	1169
ACT III—Wagnerian Singers and Orchestra.	9265-9269
DIE WALKÜRE (Wagner) Wagnerian Singers and Orchestra.	9164-9170, 9171-9177
HERODIADE—Il est doux, il est bon (Massenet)—Jeritza.	6604

QUESTIONS

1. In what century and under what conditions was the opera *Dafne* written? What period of time had elapsed since the *first* effort in writing opera?

2. What were the characteristics of Italian music and in what ways did they differ from the French ideals of opera?

3. Who was Christopher Gluck? How did he influence the development of opera?

4. Name three of the famous Italian operas of the nineteenth century. Name three French operas of the same period.

5. Who was the most radical reformer of opera in the nineteenth century? Outline briefly his life and accomplishments.

6. Explain what is meant by the *Leit-motif*.

Chapter VIII

BEETHOVEN, SCHUBERT, SCHUMANN AND LISZT

We have now reached the period of the *Romantic* movement in music. The common tendency of the Romanticists was the search for the spiritual element in the national life. They buried themselves in mediaeval romances, in the ideals of chivalry and monasticism, and in folk lore. With eyes turned upon German landscape and German common life, they saw them not as they really are, but transfigured by the mists of fantasy.

It was Beethoven who opened the gates to this new movement. The commanding position which Beethoven holds in the history of art cannot be stated in a single formula. He does not belong wholly either to the eighteenth or to the nineteenth century, but in his works of different periods can be found the controlling ideas of both. In some of his works there is conformity to a type, in others defiant assertion of individualism. The classic sonata form which Haydn established, you remember, attained in Beethoven its complete maturity of outline and content. He revealed its full possibilities as a means of characteristic expression.

Beethoven was born in 1770 at the little town of Bonn, on the Rhine. His parents were miserably poor, and his father, bearing in mind that Mozart had made great sums of money by giving concerts while a mere child, decided that his son should do likewise. And so at the age of six Ludwig was made to enter upon a rigorous course of musical training, planned and at first conducted by his father. The father's main object being the earliest and greatest development of his son's musical genius so as to make it a "marketable commodity," he gave him no other education than that afforded by public schools.

When he was twenty-two years of age Beethoven went to Vienna. There he attracted attention first by

BEETHOVEN (1770-1827)

80

the force and magnetism of his piano-playing, especially in improvising. In general, he was appreciated and encouraged as a composer, but his development at last outran the taste of the public.

As we have said, the historical significance of Beethoven lies in the fact that he marks the transition from the eighteenth century to the nineteenth. Let us here examine a part of one of his first sonatas:

Sonata

L. van BEETHOVEN, Op. 2, Nº 1
(1770-1827)

This first selection is a striking example of the classic period in Beethoven's work. The sonata from which it is taken was composed about 1795-96, before the vigorous, romantic spirit had taken hold on the composer. The theme, as you see, is plain and unemotional. There is nothing in it to excite the imagination; it does not suggest any particular mood which the composer wanted to express. As the sonata continues, the theme is taken up and developed—ingeniously but without any attempt to convey emotional ideas. The whole aim of the sonata, in short, is to conform to an abstract and generalized type or form of music.

As he matured intellectually and musically, however, Beethoven began to tend away from the classic ideal. His music, more than that of his predecessors, took on a tender and emotional turn. He sought more and more to express individual feeling. And finally, when his new ideals brought him into conflict with certain traditions of musical form, he defied the traditions and wrote passionately, with absolute freedom of expression. In so doing he caught the whole revolutionary spirit of nineteenth century art.

The next selection, taken from the introduction of a sonata written in 1820, presents a very different type of music from that of the classic example previously quoted:

Almost without playing this selection, you can see that it is unlike the selection preceding; the very notes on the page look different. And as you play these measures, you observe that there is a peculiar agitation about them. They have nothing of that smooth, almost mechanical regularity of the classical fragment quoted above. They have a sort of nervous restlessness, as though the composer were trying to tell something about his own mood. The same idea persists in the following measures from the same introduction:

Then presently there enters into the music this bit of melody, as if the vague emotions which mark the earlier passages were beginning to take on a definite form and find a clearer expression:

Immediately after the introduction comes the theme of the first movement.

It suggests a strong, determined activity—the setting in motion of great forces. The spirit of it is like the spirit of the Crusaders when they rode forth to conquer the Saracen. To be sure, the theme does not actually represent a Crusade or any other particular action; we cannot say, "Now the gates are thrown open; now the horsemen ride through." But it does express a mood. We can feel certain that when Beethoven wrote it, he was not thinking of rippling brooks or shepherds playing their pipes on the hillside. The mood is serious and courageous—perhaps even a little grim.

Between these two extreme types of sonata illustrated above —the one distinctly classic and the other distinctly romantic— lie many others of Beethoven's sonatas in which the classic and the romantic were peculiarly blended. It is, then, both because his very early works were typically classical and his very late works typically romantic, and because his intervening works contained side by side traces of the classic and traces of the romantic, that we speak of Beethoven as representing a transition between the eighteenth and nineteenth century composers.

In Beethoven's melody the Italian influence is seen profoundly modified and deepened. Everywhere in his work is perceptible the immense enlargement of expression. Equal advance is shown in his harmony—in its massiveness and richness, as well as in his fondness for abrupt changes and modulations and harsh dissonances.

Beethoven, like Wagner, who studied him so eagerly, never wrote for the "galleries"; he was ever true to his ideals. And he must be regarded as one of the pivotal figures in all musical development. His death occurred in 1827, when he was fifty-seven years of age.

Early in the nineteenth century the German song for single voice—the *Lied*, as it was called—with piano accompaniment, achieved its fixed position among the historical musical forms. Its previous condition had been one of humility, beloved by the common people, but hardly noticed by the leading composers. The rise of the art song in the case of Schubert, Schumann, and others was one of the inevitable consequences of the new romantic movement. The expansion of the Lied into its present scope is the work, before all others, of Franz Schubert.

SCHUBERT AND HIS FRIENDS

The Lied is distinguished from the earlier forms of solo song (such as the Italian aria) in this respect—that no longer the music, but the *word-text* appears as the chief element. The composer seeks by his art to enhance the effect of the poet's words. The complete model for this phase of art was once for all established by Schubert.

Schubert's life was obscure and uneventful. He was born in a suburb of Vienna in 1797. After he was grown he lived a precarious and somewhat Bohemian existence in Vienna, frequently pinched by poverty and hampered by lack of recognition. No composition of his was published until 1821. From that time, Schubert's reputation grew steadily, and he was about to enter upon a career of distinction when a fever snatched him away at the age of thirty-one.

As an example of Schubert's work we may take his song *The Erlking,* of which the words were written by Johann Wolfgang von Goethe, the celebrated German poet. In order to understand the music more clearly, let us study the following brief outline of the poem. While riding through a furious storm the father seeks to quiet the fears of his young son, who cries repeatedly that the Erlking, who symbolizes death, is luring him away. Becoming more insistent, the Erlking threatens to take the child by force. Pressing on through the tempest the father arrives home, only to find the child dead in his arms.

The introductory measures of the song establish at once its dramatic atmosphere. They depict the fury of the storm. In the following passage, especially in the peculiar figure which runs through the bass, we can hear the rushing wind, carrying with it something hostile, menacing.

The Erlking

FRANZ SCHUBERT

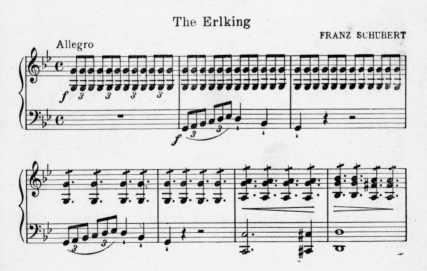

In that manner the accompaniment continues up to the point where the Erlking pleads with the child to come with him, promising that his daughters will sing and rock him to sleep each night. During this passage the accompaniment has the swaying motion of a cradle. As soon as the Erlking ceases the boy cries out to his father in terror, and the accompaniment is again stormy, fateful.

At the end the storm dies suddenly away. The voice tells us very simply that the child is dead, after which the accompaniment sets its seal with two chords.

The Erlking is commonly recognized as the most remarkable ballad song in all musical literature. In many minds the term "ballad" is associated with sentimental love-lyrics but strictly it should apply only to narrative songs. *The Erlking* is a story, related not only by the words but also in the vivid accompaniment.

The vogue for Romantic music did not exercise its sway over all the composers of that time. In Hamburg in the year 1809, was born one who was destined to be a famous musician, but a musician who reverted to the classical style. It was Felix Mendelssohn, the grandson of a philosopher and the son of a rich banker. His musical education was based on Bach, Handel, Haydn and Mozart, and his tendency in composition was to recall what he considered the too radical taste of his time to the solid in substance and traditionally regular in form. His music in its untroubled serenity, its perfect finish of detail, its grace and melodious quality gave him a great vogue. His *Songs Without Words* were long on every piano, his oratorio *Elijah* rivals *The Messiah* in popularity, and his *Midsummer Night's Dream* overture written when he was but seventeen has a freshness, charm and spontaneity that gives it a unique place in music.

The qualities expressed in his music are a reflection of his untroubled, happy life. (Felix means happy.) He was not plunged into distressing circumstances, his heart and mind were not torn by sorrows for which he wished to find relief in music, as did Beethoven. Mendelssohn's life was a tranquil one, his wealthy parents were of high social position, he was well educated, and his marriage was happy.   In such a peaceful environment did he not have every inducement to write music that was as unharrassed and polished as his own life?

He was a devout student of Bach and in Leipzig gave the first performance of the great *St. Matthew Passion* which had been given since Bach's death.   He was also the founder in 1843 of the Leipzig Conservatory of Music, so long the center of musical education in Germany.

Mendelssohn was one of the few composers to achieve great success during his lifetime.   His ceaseless activity coupled with overwork and the sudden death of his favorite sister brought his precocious life to a close on Nov. 4, 1847.

Another romantic composer belonging to the first half of the nineteenth century was Robert Schumann, who was born at Zwickau, Saxony, in 1810.   His songs stand second to none in richness and mellow poetic feeling.   Inferior to Schubert in melodic invention, he relied for expression more upon harmony and rhythm, and indeed his accompaniments are often more important than the voice parts.

But it is in Schumann's piano pieces that we find his most marked contributions to musical progress.   His use of the chord

is massive—often extending beyond an octave, and his compositions are notable for variety, originality of rhythm, and almost excessive use of syncopations.   Furthermore, by ingenious management of the pedal he secured effects that had never previously been attained.

Schumann frequently used poetic titles for his pieces.   He found an inspiration to musical creation in definite, describable situations drawn from external life and the inner world of emotion.   He paused at the

SCHUMANN (1810-1856)

threshold of "programme" music.   His pieces did not depict a succession of scenes, but were strongly descriptive of moods.

Let us consider his *Carnaval*.   What does the name suggest? A brilliant scene of shifting colors, varied types of people, some careless, some whimsical, some meditative, but almost all in an atmosphere of gayety and keen interest in life.   The *Carnaval* is divided into a series of small pieces depicting the above phases

Mr. Cross - many absolute determination, of style and beauty and force of the true carnival spirit. Take, for instance, the one entitled *Pierrot*. Pierrot is a clown walking along the midway, looking at everything but the road over which he is walking. Of course you know what happens when one does that—one stumbles. That is what happened to the clown. You will find Schumann's music for that situation on this and the following page.

Carnaval

(Pierrot)

Schumann's career, though brilliant, was comparatively short. He died in 1856, before he had fairly entered on middle age.

A contemporary of Schumann who likewise devoted himself to the piano was the Polish genius, Frédéric Chopin. He seemed to have been born with an innate instinct for the piano, and he is one of the few who have gained a place in the first rank of composers by virtue of work along one line of composition. Except for a small group of songs, Chopin wrote only for the piano. He is known as the "Poet of the Piano" and for his beloved instrument developed a new and individual idiom. His writing is never polyphonic but always accompanied melody in which he strikes a happy mean between sentiment and sentimentality.

Chopin was the first to introduce the Slavonic element into music. His Mazurkas and Polonaises are idealizations of national dances. A marked characteristic of his works is their flowing continuity. A recent French work* compares this quality of Chopin's music and its balanced rhythm, to the onward surge of the ocean. "There comes a wave, another and perhaps another, then the rushing forward of the water high upon the beach after which it falls back again. Chopin had a trick of introducing a motif, repeating it once or oftener, then plunging into a longer passage finally returning to his motif." Is not that like the ocean?

FRÉDÉRIC CHOPIN, Op. 66

Chopin was born near Warsaw, Feb. 22, 1810. In 1831 he went to Paris where he lived until his death, Oct. 17, 1849.

The outcome of the romantic movement was the "programme" school. The composer of "programme music" selects a poem, a narrative, or a series of scenes, or invents them for himself, and then writes a piece of music which reflects the successive pictures of episodes. Perhaps on the printed programme at the concert will be a description of the story the music tells, but the school derives its name of "programme" music from the series of visions or mental changes which the music illustrates.

At the head of this school stands Franz Liszt, who was born in Hungary, in 1811. In versatility and all-around practical capacity, Liszt may be considered as having exerted the most compelling personal influence of his time. He was great as composer, pianist, conductor and teacher. Indeed, not only was he one of the greatest pianists in history, but the whole school of piano playing at the present day takes its style and direction from him.

Liszt was essentially Hungarian in his music and his rhapsodies and many other works brought the Magyar folk-music into

*See *La Musique et la Vie Intericure,* by Lucien Bourguès et Alexandre Denéréaz, page 434.

the modern concert répertoire.   His Hungarian rhapsodies were responsible for a new spirit in music.   The themes and many of the rhythms are native; the harmonies and decoration, while characteristically Liszt's, are at the same time modelled after those of the Gypsy performers.   Liszt intended them as a sort of national epic, instrumental ballads in which the spirit and the peculiar mode of expression of an interesting people are reflected.

FRANZ LISZT (1811-1886)

In his wholly original compositions are shown his love of nature, literature and art, and often his religious feeling, which was very deep.   Liszt's transcriptions of songs and orchestral pieces are poetical resettings, seen through the medium of the piano.   In the "symphonic poem," Liszt contributed a new form.   The symphonic poem is a work in a single movement, in which sometimes a continuous series of ideas or occurrences is illustrated by the music, and sometimes a single conception is revealed in changing lights.

Liszt was the most phenomenal pianist that ever existed.   He conceived technic as a means of expression.   His inspiration was the thought of bringing the capacity of the piano as near as possible to that of the violin, the voice and the orchestra.   His transcriptions were largely designed to reveal the higher powers of the piano, which he was the first to divine.   He learned for himself and taught the world that the fascinations of a supreme technic do not alone satisfy; the pianist, like any other artist, must appeal to the intellect and the emotional sensibility.

The greatest of technicians, he was also the first and still remains the greatest of the modern school of emotional "dramatic" performers, whose aim is to reveal all the possibilities of beauty in the works of the great composers.   Liszt died at Bayreuth in 1886, at the age of seventy-five.

He was remarkable not only as a pianist of supreme gift, a composer of original conception, a conductor of rare insight and a teacher of world-wide influence, but was equally remarkable as a whole-souled, generous man, utterly free from envy. No great musician ever did so much to befriend and encourage his fellow musicians.

Let us compare a Hungarian folksong, as it is sung by the Gypsies, with one of Liszt's rhapsodies. Here is the folksong, called *Moonlight and Starry Night.** Notice particularly the elaborate ornamentation which is added to the melody—the groups of small notes which do nothing but enrich the general effect. The melody itself, as you see, is plaintive folksong and comparatively simple.

Hungarian Folksong
Arranged by Lajor Serly

Poor, un-worth-y I of dream - ing   Dreams, love, of you.

Nay, by moon-light   or by star - light,   I can-not dream

*From *Folksongs of many People.* Copyrighted by *The Womans Press*; and published here with permission.

Following is a passage from Liszt's *13th Hungarian Rhapsody*. Again we have the simple melody lavishly embroidered with arpeggios and runs. Liszt has thus preserved faithfully the distinguishing characteristic of Hungarian folk music.

We have now reached strictly modern music. In the next chapter we shall consider the tendencies of music at the present time, and particularly the influence of the old folksongs on some of the great compositions of today.

The following phonograph records may be used to illustrate some of the musical selections in this chapter.

Title	Victor Record No.
CORIOLAN OVERTURE (Beethoven)—London Symphony Orchestra. See list of records in Chapter I.	9279
HUNGARIAN FANTASIE (based on gypsy folk tunes) (Liszt)— Royal Albert Hall Orchestra.	
Part I and Part II.	9110
Part III and Part IV.	9111
LES PRÉLUDES (*Symphonic Poem*) (Liszt)—San Francisco Symphony Orchestra.	6863-6864
AVE MARIA (Schubert)—Heifetz.	6691
THE ERLKING (Schubert)—Jeritza.	6704
TWO GRENADIERS (Schumann)—Chaliapin.	6619
QUARTET, F MAJOR (Beethoven)—Busch Quartet.	M-206
SYMPHONY No. 9 (Beethoven) Coates—Symphony Orchestra	9061-9068
ROSAMUNDE—Entr'acte (Schubert) San Francisco Symphony Orchestra.	6678
UNFINISHED SYMPHONY (Schubert) Philadelphia Symphony Orchestra.	6663-6665
MIDSUMMER NIGHT'S DREAM—(Mendelssohn) San Francisco Symphony Orchestra.	6675-6678
EVENING SONG (Schumann) Victor String Ensemble.	19854
TWENTY-FOUR PRELUDES (Chopin) Cortot.	6715-6718

Title	Victor Record No.
IT WAS A LOVER AND HIS LASS (Shakespeare-Morley) ; LONGING FOR SPRING (Mozart) ; MARMOTTE (Beethoven).	24788A
SONGS WITHOUT WORDS (Mendelssohn).	24797A
QUINTETTE, OP. 44 (1st mvt.) ; QUARTET (Scherzo) (Schumann).	24798B
FAR ABOVE US FLIES THE HERON (Hungarian Gypsy).	24782B

QUESTIONS

1. Why is Beethoven spoken of as representing the transitional period between the eighteenth and nineteenth century composers?

2. What musical form established by Haydn was carried to completion by Beethoven?

3. Tell the story of *The Erlking*. By whom was it written? In what respects is it remarkable?

4. Tell what you can of Schumann's music. How does it differ from Schubert's?

5. What is "programme" music?

6. Explain briefly the important features of the work of Franz Liszt.

Chapter IX

MODERN MUSIC

Music is peculiarly the outgrowth of the generation to which it belongs. Every period has had its musical fashions. There is a general opinion that modern music is degenerating. When it is compared with the music of the Romantic and Classical periods, which is considered beautiful, the music of today, which sounds so different, is called ugly. We forget that each composer who introduced a new musical idea was considered a "modernist." It would be impossible for a composer of today to produce the music which Bach did, and it would be equally impossible for Bach to produce today the music he did in the seventeenth century.

As early as the sixteenth century composers began to have a feeling for tonality. *Tonality* is the sense of key relationship. Every key has other keys related to it. Let us study the scale of *Do* (C) major.

Do (C) is the *key-note*, or *tonic*, of this scale. It is the *tonality* which our ears recognize as the satisfying conclusion. Play the first seven notes of the above scale and stop. Are you satisfied? No, the ear demands another note and one will be humming it even before that eighth note is played, the tonic *Do*, which establishes the tonality of this scale.

To find the keys attendant on the key of *Do* count five notes above *Do*, and five below, thus,

Fa (f) and *Sol* (g) may be the tonic notes of two new major scales. Divide the scale of *Do* in half. There are two groups of four notes each. Going down from the *Do* of the first group the scale of *Fa* (F) major is obtained, and building up from the *Do* of the second group the scale of *Sol* (G) major is formed. The *lower*

part of the *original* scale forms the *upper* part of the *new* scale, just as the *upper* part of the *original* scale forms the *lower* part of *another* new scale, as in the following:

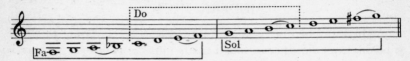

Each major key has its related key which is the *parallel minor*. This may be found by counting down one whole and one half tone (a "minor third") from the major tonic note. There are three kinds of *minor scales:* (1) *antique*, (2) *melodic* and (3) *harmonic*. The last is the one most used for it has the same notes as its relative major except that the seventh note is raised one half tone. The last attendant key of the major scale is its tonic minor. So, there are six keys which are related to the key of *Do* major: (1) *Fa* (F); (2) *Sol* (G) major; (3) the tonic minor *do* (c)*; (4) the relative minor of *Do* which is *La* (a) minor; (5) the relative minor of *Fa*, which is *re* (d) minor; and (6) *Sol* which is *mi* (e) minor. This method of finding its attendant keys may be applied to any major scale.

The minor scale cannot be divided into halves like the major scale, to make two more minor scales, because of the raised seventh note, which makes it impossible for the original scale to remain unaltered. The attendant keys, however, can be found by the same method as those of the major scale. Thus every *major scale* has the following six attendant keys: its own relative and tonic minor keys; its fifth above and fifth below and their relative minor keys. Every *minor scale* has for its attendant keys its own relative and tonic major keys; its fifth above and below and their relative major keys.

Example of scale of *La* minor and Attendant Keys:

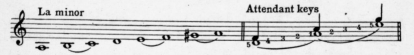

The relative major keys are indicated by the small quarter notes.

A composition written with due regard to tonality may have

*It should be noted the capital letters are used in music to indicate major scales and small letters for the minor scales.

modulations into distant keys, but they are not dwelt upon. The composer quickly passes into a key which is related to the tonic key. Turn back to the illustrations from Beethoven's *Fifth Symphony* in the first chapter. The Symphony opens in the tonic key *c* minor. The third illustration ends in *E*♭ major, the relative major of *c* minor. The fourth illustration is in *f* minor. And so on through the first movement. Beethoven never forgot that *c* minor was his tonic key and did not harass our ears by writing in a key alien to *c* minor.

It may be inquired why it is called the Symphony in *C* minor when the second movement is written in *A*♭ major, the third movement in *c* minor and the fourth in *C* major. A composition is always called by the tonic key in which it begins and the other movements are usually written in a key related to the tonic key. Another characteristic of a composition which is written with due regard for tonality is that only *one key at a time* is used. Another study of the illustrations from Beethoven's Symphony makes clear that the key of *c* minor is heard alone, that of *E*♭ major alone, and *f* minor alone. Though he modulated into many other keys, Beethoven did not write in more than one key at the same time.

Today we have *poly-tonality* which means the use of *more* than one key at a time. Many compositions which sound very complicated and more or less excruciating to the ears would sound quite simple if written in one tonality. Try the four measures below and observe that the bass is written in *f* minor and the treble in *f sharp* minor.

Botafogo

DARIUS MILHAUD

And now try them written in the one key, *f* minor.

This piece is written in the simple three-part song-form.

It is one of the weaknesses of poly-tonality that if the piece is played in *one* tonality it loses its bizarre sound and becomes something very commonplace. It requires no inspiration, no great musical talent, but only a little ingenuity, to achieve unusual effects by writing a piece in two tonalities at the same time. A weird harmonization sometimes covers up a poverty of musical ideas.

Another tendency of modern music is to be *rhythmical* rather than *metrical*. In *metrical music* the accent of the rhythm is confined strictly within the bars of each measure, there are regular marked accents in every measure, and the same rhythm is maintained through all, or nearly all, the composition. But in *rhythmical music* the composer either changes the measure signature at the beginning of practically every measure, or he leaves out the bars entirely. In the latter case one must sense the pulsation of the rhythm and place the accents where they will best bring out the meaning of the music. It is like finding the accented word in a sentence which will give expression to the phrase. Below is a portion of Palmgren's *Isle of Shadows*. It is written without measure signature, but the lightly sketched measure bars and signatures show where the pulsations occur.

Isle of Shadows

Lack of melody in the new music is deplored by many. When certain scales, known centuries ago to primitive men, were revived by Debussy, new fields of harmonization were opened. Composers, adopting these new scales, lost sight of melody written for its own sake which is easily caught by the ear so that the hearer may whistle it. But melodies were, and are, written and harmonized in such a way that they are not easily recognizable as melodies by untrained ears.

One scale which is in much use in modern music is the *whole tone scale.* This scale is so called because there are no half-steps in it. Begin on any note and play seven succeeding notes spaced a whole step apart. The *chromatic scale,* too, is popular. To build this latter scale, begin on any note and proceed by successive half-steps. It is easy to see how the use of these scales must immediately break the conventional methods of harmonization since they do not remain in one tonality. Indeed, the use of them has led to *atonality* in some instances—a complete lack of any tonic key.

The Gargoyle

EUGENE GOOSENS

It must be remembered that many of the compositions which are being written today are *experiments*, not finished products. Musicians are trying out new tone-effects to see what can be done with them. It is like learning a new language. Only gradually and after much practice can fluency and colloquialism be acquired. The modern composers are, as a rule, very strict in their regard of form.   Indeed, there is a tendency to return more and more to the classical style of composition of the eighteenth century. The personal and emotional elements are being repressed and music for itself alone is being written.   Many composers are aiming at realism too (see page 103).   They attempt to describe objects and their movements through the medium of music.

The school of Modern Music in general is a direct outgrowth of the Romantic school.   It may be said that as Richard Wagner's works mark the highest achievement of the Romantic school and are the foundation of modern opera, so the works of Franz Liszt stand in the same relation to instrumental music.

With the exception of Brahms, the greatest modern German master, and his followers, all modern composers of instrumental and operatic music have founded their work on the two basic principles of the Romantic school—programme music and nationality.   Brahms did not carry on the traditions of the romantic and programme periods.   He was more nearly a classicist, but one of a period of time when life was more intense than in the eighteenth century.   He was not a spontaneous composer; his works were wrought with the greatest regard for musical science.   His style is sonorous, broad, and generally intricate in harmony and rhythm.   But he was also capable of utmost simplicity.   His symphonies reveal a new fund of beauties on each hearing.   His songs are among the most beautiful written.   His *Lullaby* is perhaps one of the best known melodies.   It has the style of a simple folk song. In the music of Brahms one finds the beauty and warmth of a fine mind and complete emotional restraint.

We already know what is meant by *programme music*; we know that it is music written to depict a series of scenes, events or incidents.   But what do we mean by nationality?   Ever since the writing of music became a consciously developed art, there have been certain traits, certain characteristics in the music of any one nation or any one race which distinguish it from the music of any other.   Thus the Italians, as we have seen, early became identified with sweetness of melody; the Germans with massive chords and rich harmonies; and the French with distinctive rhythms.   The Romanticists and musicians of the modern school have not only respected these national peculiarities, but have sought eagerly to define and to emphasize them.   By studying the folk tunes of their own people, some of the best modern composers have been able to catch a genuine national spirit and incorporate it into their own works. In doing so they have given music as a whole a new interest and a new vitality.

A German of today who has pushed the programme method to its farthest limits is Richard Strauss whose orchestral works precipitated a controversy but little less violent than the works of Wagner. Strauss began his career with pieces for orchestra and chamber music that followed the classic traditions, but in 1885 he turned toward the literalism of programme music. Since then his music has seemed to express an insatiable desire for new sensations. He portrays the ugly as well as the beautiful. For instance, in his *Salomé*, at the moment of the beheading of John the Baptist, the music simulates the sawing of a knife, and in *Elektra* he brings in the lashing of whips. Strauss has spared no pains to be literal and whatever picture he strove to paint he has made most vivid through his amazing technical resource.

His unique position was established by his symphonic poems, among which are *Death and Transfiguration, Thus Spake Zarathustra, Don Quixote,* and others. He gave the symphonic poem form and careful construction. He took the precaution to select programmes which would conform to a musical structure. Heretofore this form of music had been free and loose, but he made it concrete and logically connected. Strauss must also be rated among the foremost song writers of his time for some of his Lieder are of the first order in respect to beauty and poetic insight. He was born in Munich, Jan. 11, 1864.

The music produced on French soil has always had a decidedly national flavor; its vitality has never been exhausted; and in no country at the present day is musical energy more active, ambitious, and individual. At the same time there is always to be found in France a marked tendency toward the programme type of music. The French mind is disinclined to think abstractly. It demands words, a subject, a story, a definite hint of some kind to stimulate the fancy and give a picturesque character to the composition. Those qualities of picturesqueness and nationality, combined with a newly awakened interest in purely instrumental music, may be said to dominate the newer school of French musical art, out of which have developed many of the outstanding masterpieces in modern instrumental music.

The true founder of the modern French school was César Franck (1822-1890), whose entire life was given to the cause of developing French instrumental music. He was a beloved and able teacher, and a composer whose works include many beautiful songs, symphonic poems, one of the greatest of modern symphonies, and pieces for the organ and piano.

His music shows the influence of many composers whom he admired, among them Liszt, who was his friend and played his music, and Wagner whose use of the *chromatic scale* (see page 101 and examples in *Tristan and Isolde* page 76) haunted him. Franck made extensive use of chromaticism. He frequently accompanied chromatics with the whole tone scale, a combination rich in beauty. In his longer compositions, as in his *Symphony in D*, Franck built up his design through a cyclic use of themes. The themes which were introduced in the first movement and which formed integral parts of the second and third movements, were woven into many patterns, making a most complete whole. The freedom of harmonization which Franck acquired was one of his greatest contributions to music.

Until his recent death the senior among great modern French composers was Camille Saint-Saëns (1835-1921), who wrote a great number of works in all forms—piano, organ, symphonies, concertos, symphonic poems, and operas.

The most unique genius of the modern French school was Claude Debussy (1862-1920), whose rare combinations of instrumental effects are absolutely original in the world of music. Not only did he make use of the old scales, but also of consecutive fifths which were used in the tenth century. He said this idea came to him at the Paris exposition in 1900 on hearing musicians from the Far East. He and his followers are of the newer group, who seek new fields of expression by means of adventurous, free and wholly individual uses of harmony, rhythm and tone color. This movement, which is active in every musical country, arises from the characteristic desire of the age to let music express everything that it is capable of expressing, and also from the fact that the human ear becomes, as time goes on, trained to appreciate finer and more complex musical combinations.

Thoroughly romantic in temperament, a passionate lover of nature, Debussy drew his material from picturesque fancy, from delicate moods of nature, even from the odd creatures of fairy-tale and myth. The poets whom he has chosen for illustration in his songs, opera, and instrumental tone poems are the fantastic idealists—Rossetti, Maeterlinck, and Mallarmé for example. Debussy was thus akin in sympathy to the "impressionist" painters, who sacrifice drawing to shimmering effects of light, and to the "symbolist" writers, who use words not for exact portrayal, but for suggestion by means of sound and association.

His style being adapted only to a certain order of ideas, Debussy wisely made no attempt to employ it for subjects to which it was unsuited. The natural objects he strove to portray are clouds, the sea, calm or running waters; the emotions he loved to depict are the most exquisite impressions and intimate unrealized longings. He has written piano pieces, songs, orchestral works, string quartets, and the opera *Pelléas et Mélisande*, based on a remarkable drama by Maeterlinck. This opera is perhaps his most important work.

Debussy's music shows the influence of the Russian school. When quite young he spent some time in Russia where he yielded to the charms of the curious modulations of the music of the Russian people. In *Pelléas* there are passages which bring to mind Moussorgsky's *Boris Godunov*. Debussy was, however, more subtle and far more self-controlled than Moussorgsky. He preferred under-expression to the unpolished frankness of the Russian.

A characteristic bit of Debussy's music is given here. It is from a piece called *The Little Shepherd*. If you are not used to the Debussy style, you probably will not like it at first. The tone combinations will be very likely to sound freakish and harsh to you. But after you become accustomed to them, you will realize their delicate charm; you will hear the little shepherd piping a plaintive tune as he watches the sheep; you will catch the whole pastoral spirit which Debussy strove to express.

The Little Shepherd

In 1875 was born Ravel who is one of the most important of the modern French composers. He is hardly second to Debussy, but his music—while underlaid by the poetic idea—is more acid, less sentimental than that of Debussy. He does not employ the whole-tone scale to such an extent. He understands the music of other people and of other times, and likes to interpret it in his own inimitable way. He writes Spanish and Gypsy music, and music in the style of the eighteenth century. After the Great War, he wrote a suite called *The Tomb of Couperin*, each piece of which is dedicated to a friend who was lost at the Front. The Suite is written in the style of Couperin.

There gathered together in France six young composers who were disciples of Erik Satie. They became exponents of the most ultra-modern in music. Satie, whose lead they followed, seems, to many, to have written music with no particular meaning behind it, seems to have deliberately sought to bewilder the public. Jean-Aubrey in his sketch of Satie, which is included in his book *French Music of Today*, says that Satie became interested at a very early

age in early medieval church music; that Satie, far from composing with the one idea of bewildering the public, wrote with strict
self-discipline and application. He wrote in threes in order to
test the measure of his success. There are three *Sarabands,* three
Gymnopédies, etc. In the latter he confined himself to the slow
forms of Spartan and sacred dances. Under his observance of
old forms seethed a lively sense of humor which began to show
itself in his music. One set of pieces he called *Cold Pieces,*
another, *Pieces in the Shape of a Pear.* This humor is difficult
to comprehend and has given rise to much criticism.

The six avowed followers of Satie are: Milhaud, Honegger,
Poulenc, Germaine Tailleferre, Durey and Auric. Honegger has
gone farthest of all. He studied Bach, Wagner, Strauss, and from
them learned the value of discipline and sound technique in composition. He is a contra-puntalist. He has written many kinds of
music — operas, ballets, symphonies. He is particularly successful in such compositions as *Rugby,* the description of a football
game, and *Pacific 2-3-1,* the description of a powerful locomotive
in action. The latter is realism in the *nth* degree, vivid, stirring.
This realism of Honegger is not expressed in a mere jumble of
dissonances which utterly confuse the listener. On the contrary,
it is clearly defined, full of rhythm and music.

Milhaud had not the instinctive musical ability of Honegger.
Nor does he seem to have the imagination. His music gives an
impression of having been thought out deliberately, and he has
used polytonality generously.

All six of these young composers care little for sentiment.
They follow the general tendency to simplify music, leave out personalities, emotions, to—in short—revert to the severely classical
style of the *eighteenth* century.

Albert Roussel is another contemporary French composer
who, older than the *Six,* is developing an independent musical per-
sonality. Among his compositions are *Évocations* and *Pour une
Fête de Printemps.* He is a great lover of nature, as his music
testifies. It has been said of him that his art is that of a landscape
painter.*

There are still evidences of the influence of the seventeenth
century in Italian music today. Teutonic influence has had little

*Jean-Aubrey: *French Music of Today.*

effect here. But in the general mind Italian music is associated with opera. Verdi and Puccini are the composers in that line whose names rank first in Italy. Indeed Puccini (1858-1924) is the foremost Italian composer of opera today. His reputation has reached its height in the operas *La Bohème* (1897), *Tosca* (1900), and *Madame Butterfly* (1904). The last named work has made an especial appeal to the world by reason of the delicacy and beauty with which the touching history of the deceived and forsaken Japanese girl is treated by the composer.

Three musicians of Italy who are today well-known outside of their own country are Malipiero, Respighi and Casella. Malipiero follows the very modern impressionistic school but he also delves into the past, as is witnessed by his *La Cimarosiana,*—five pieces by Cimarosa, a composer of the eighteenth century, which Malipiero has re-orchestrated. Respighi is a musician of sound worth. His symphonic poem, *Le Fontane di Roma* so vividly describes the old fountains in Rome that one can hear the water as it sprays forth. As a contrast to this, there is his orchestral suite, *Four Ancient Dances.* These four dances were originally associated with the Lute in the sixteenth and seventeenth centuries. In Respighi's orchestration, the spirit of that time is retained. Casella is well-known in this country as a conductor. As a composer he has varied interests. One of them is to present different composers in his own way. One such interpretation is his *Grazioso,* a tribute to Chopin, the likeness of which to Chopin's *A major Prelude* is easily traceable.

The Italian genius is for melody and clarity. Today there is noticeable a return to the less sophisticated music of the past— in harmony, to the church modes, and, in form, to the suite of dances.

In Russia, Bohemia and Scandinavia there has long been evidence of musical vitality, but until a comparatively recent date those countries were under the influence of the older musical nations, producing music that was not national, but an echo of Italy or Germany. Now, however, they are turning towards their own native music—the folksong and folk-dance—finding there new sources of inspiration as well as new musical combinations, rhythms and melodic forms. These nations are richly endowed with racy and individual forms of folk-music, and from these and from the peculiar qualities of their national instruments they have brought into current European music certain very marked and original features.

Among the new national schools the later Russian holds an especially conspicuous place. The relation of art to national life is nowhere more apparent than in Russia, for just as the people's voice is heard in Russia's powerful and gloomy literature, so likewise a tone of struggle is perceptible in its music, a consciousness of undeveloped strength, an uncertainty as to what direction shall be taken when this strength is at last set free. Russia is searching for the native materials that shall give her music an individuality gratifying to the national pride.

No country is richer in folksongs than Russia; and another important feature of Russian national music is the music of the church. Instruments have never been allowed to be used in worship, not even the organ. Much of the liturgical or ceremonial church music consist of chants in a style somewhat similar to the Gregorian chant, reaching back with but slight modification to the earliest annals of the church.

The first Russian composer to recognize the possibilities offered by the music of his native land was Michael Glinka (1803-1857). He gave his people their first opera *A Life for the Czar*, which was produced in 1836.

Glinka broke the spell of the dominance of foreign music over Russia. His opera, which was based on a national subject and made extensive use of Russian and Polish types of melody, awoke the people to the fact that Russia was itself a treasure house of music well worth exploitation. Hitherto secular cultivated music in this country has been controlled by first Italian, then French, influences.

Following Glinka came five young men who grouped themselves under the name of "Neo-Russian" school. They laid down rules for the development of purely Russian music based on Russian folkmusic. This group of five consisted of Alexander Borodin (1834-1887), Mili Balakirev (1837-1910), Cesar Cui (1835-1918), Modeste Moussorgsky (1839-1886), and Nicolas Rimsky-Korsakov (1844-1908). Unfortunately, these talented young men, with one exception, looked down upon a knowledge of the technique of composition. They believed that in learning rules of harmony, orchestration, and the fundamentals of good music all originality and national flavor were lost. Rimsky-Korsakov alone realized the wisdom of rules. He studied and acquired a culture which saved him from the defects which his comrades did not always escape. He revised many of their compositions, among them Moussorgsky's opera *Boris Godounov.* It is this version which is usually performed today.

The "Five" drew upon the peculiar rhythms and melodies of the Russian folkmusic for their inspiration. Moussorgsky's music is held as highly representative of the national spirit.

TCHAIKOVSKY (1840-1893)

From one of Moussorgsky's works, *The Song of the Flea,* two sections are given on page 111. The song itself is a droll affair telling of a certain king who once took a great fancy to a flea. Inviting the insect to court, he had it dressed in fine clothes and honored with official titles. The flea returned the compliment by bringing with it all its relatives, much to the discomfort of the courtiers, who were forbidden by royal mandate to kill the pests or even to scratch the bites. The idea for the song was taken from Goethe's dramatic poem *Faust;* but Moussorgsky's music is thoroughly Russian in spirit.

Important among later composers are Anton Rubinstein (1830-1894), Peter Tchaikovsky (1840-1893), and Serge Rachmaninov (1873-   ). Rubinstein was a famous pianist and an ambitious composer, but his compositions are not strictly national. Tchaikovsky, too, is not typical of Russia—is, perhaps, more German—but his music is sincere and in the expression of grief, despair, Tchaikovsky knew no limits. His *Symphonie Pathétique* is perhaps the only symphony which ends on a tragic note. Rachmaninov believes that melody is the integral foundation of all music; that it is for this reason that the great composers of the past have shown such respect for the peasant melodies of their countries.

Song of the Flea

Song of Mephistopheles in Auerbach's Cellar from Goethe's Faust

M. P. MOUSSORGSKY (1879)

Among the living Russian Composers, Stravinsky is perhaps the greatest.   He startled the world with his *Rite of Spring,* a picture of Pagan Russia.   He is quoted as saying that he wishes not to suggest situations or emotions, but to manifest them, express them; to achieve straightforward expression in its simplest form. His music is largely that of a devoted Russian nationalist.   He is not an innovator, but he used old methods in new ways.   He is absolutely unafraid of dissonant chords, but he uses them for a purpose.   There is not much atonality in his music, but a great deal of polytonality.   His use of rhythms is very clever and interesting.   He gained prominence from *The Fire Bird, Petrouchka,* and the *Rite of Spring.*   They were all three written for the Ballet. Since 1923 his interests have gone back to the severe contrapuntal style of Bach.

Among the younger composers is Prokofieff.   His compositions are more coherent than those of Milhaud, Auric, etc.   He seems to have acquired greater fluency in speaking the new musical idiom.   Other Russian musicians of today are Scriabin and Glazounov.   In the music of Scriabin can be found the influence of Wagner.   There are really three distinct periods in the life of Scriabin.   In the first, he chiefly wrote piano compositions in which he took Chopin for his model.   In the second period he wrote more for the orchestra, and at this time he followed the precepts of Wagner.   In the third division, he has become highly original, and given us a new harmonic system.   Also, at the beginning of this time he became a theosophist, and his works are based on programmes, the subjects being taken from theosophy.   His fundamental idea of music is "art as religion and religion as something involving the conception of art."*

In any broad discussion of modern music, Bohemia—once described by Wagner as "the land of harp-players and street musicians"—deserves a generous share of attention.   Indeed that strange, romantic country has always been considered one of the most musical in all Europe.   And although political misfortunes have until recently prevented the growth of a definite Bohemian "school," the town pipers and strolling musicians have

*A Great Russian Love-Poet; Scriabin by Hull.

kept alive since the fifteenth century a fine body of Bohemian folksongs.

Foremost of all Bohemian composers was Anton Dvořák (1841-1904). Born of the people, Dvořák knew thoroughly the folk material of his native land, and in his compositions he con-

ANTON DVOŘÁK (1841-1904)

stantly employed it. Without borrowing complete melodies from other songs, he caught the characteristics of melody, rhythm, and harmony peculiar to Bohemian folk music and in his own music imitated them ingeniously.

Dvořák also spent some years in this country and became very deeply interested in the negro music. He found it untainted, the natural, characteristic outgrowth of negro life on American soil. He delved deeply into the study of the music of these folk. His enthusiasm was revealed to the world by his *New World Symphony*. The main theme of the *Largo* from that Symphony is given here.

Theme of the Largo

From the New World Symphony

ANTON DVOŘÁK

If you could hear all of this Symphony you would catch themes which might make you ask: "Which song is that?" But Dvořák did not use one real negro melody; his themes are his own, but, so cleverly did he catch the spirit of the negro music, they sound like authentic negro tunes. It has been stated in print that Dvořák used negro and even Indian themes, but Mr. William Arms Fisher of Boston, a pupil of Dvořák, who attended the final rehearsal of the Symphony before its first performance in this country, states with certainty that every theme throughout the work was composed by Dvořák himself. The fact that they are so reminiscent of negro music proves how thoroughly he has caught the negro idiom.

Some of the most delightful music of recent days has come from Scandinavia,—Norway, Sweden and Denmark. The northern folksongs are of a peculiar and exquisite charm, and they have tinged all the work of the Scandinavian composers more or less, particularly since the European Romantic movement threw the attention of the art world back to the characteristic national subjects and racial feeling.

By Scandinavian music we find that we commonly mean Norwegian, for in music, both popular and artistic, Norway far excels Denmark and Sweden. Of this Norwegian group Edvard Grieg (1843-1907) was the most important figure. In spite of frequent visits to other countries Grieg retained his residence in Norway, devoting himself not only to composition but as well to the promoting of musical interests among his people. As a musical miniature painter, a creator of picturesque fancies, he has hardly had an equal since Schumann. He cultivated a peculiarly weird and vague kind of harmony and tonality, and adopted the forms and rhythms of popular dances. Particularly was he successful in casting over his work that atmosphere of mystery and melancholy which serves to bring up visions of gloomy fjords, lonely shores, and mountains, with their attendant legends of strange spirits of earth and sea. Grieg's music is no mere imitation of national strains, but is a natural mode of self expression. He was an original artist as well as a man of the people. The following selection entitled *Folksong* brings out the Scandinavian temperament as Grieg understood it.

Folksong

EDVARD GRIEG, Op. 38, № 2

From Finland comes one of the greatest of our contemporary composers: Jan Sibelius. His music is strongly nationalistic, expressing his love of the geography of his country: its lakes, forests,

desolation.   He has drawn much from the Finnish *Kalevala*—epic
— for his programmes; and also on Finnish and Scandinavian
literature.   His Symphonies are probably his most important contributions to music literature.

Musical culture among the English-speaking nations, for a
long time imperfectly developed, has begun to attain in the last
few years a new vigor.   The masses of the people are now
learning to appreciate what is best in musical art, and this
learning is being strengthened by private teaching, schools, societies and an expanding concert system.   Music is rapidly becoming
a part of popular life.   In England the high and rigid standards
set by Handel and Mendelssohn and insisted on by musical
audiences long discouraged native composers from striking out
in new and original directions.   The public refused a fair hearing
to the claims of the new Romantic school, which was revolutioniz-
ing musical thought and production in other lands.   Consequently
England has failed to build up for itself any worth-while body
of opera, symphony or piano music.

In later years, however, there has been a change for the
better.   Arthur Sullivan (1842-1900), a composer of comic oper-
ettas, of which *Pinafore* and *The Mikado* are two of the best
known, was one of the first of the modern English musicians to
gain distinction.

Following closely after Sullivan, there sprang up rapidly a
brilliant succession of English composers which has continued
without a break to the present day.   In 1857 was born Edward
Elgar, reckoned by some as the greatest of modern English musicians.   His outstanding work is an oratorio, *The Dream of
Gerontius*, but he wrote also many excellent songs with orchestral
accompaniment, and various other orchestral works of distinguished beauty.   Samuel Coleridge-Taylor, born in 1875, was
another to rank high among English musicians.   Himself a negro,
he gave to negro melodies an unusually deep and sympathetic
interpretation, and by his arrangements revealed the unusual
musical qualities which they possess.

Of the English composers now living, three especially de-

serve mention: Percy Grainger (1882), Cyril Scott (1879), and
Ralph Vaughn Williams (1872). Grainger, an Australian Eng-
lishman, now an American citizen, is notable both as a pianist and
as a composer. In the latter capacity, he has devoted much of
his time to the study and development of early English folksongs,
with the result that England has found herself much richer in
native music—music of the people—than had generally been
realized. Scott shows two points of similarity with Grainger—
ability as a pianist and a loyal interest in purely English music.
But the characteristic mark of his work is its reflection of the
new impressionistic school of music so much in vogue with the
French. Indeed his mastery of the newer musical forms and
ideas has won for him the title "The English Debussy."

Until recently Vaughn Williams has been perhaps less known
than either Cyril Scott or Percy Grainger. In 1917, however, the
publication of his *London Symphony* won him immediate attention. Since then certain of his other works have been performed
in this country as well as abroad. They consist chiefly of chamber
music and larger orchestral forms. It is interesting to note also
that Williams, as well as Scott and Grainger, has made careful
study of the old English folksongs.

As an example of modern English music, his *London Symphony* may well be chosen, both because it is very recent and

because it seeks to interpret, musically, the spirit of a great English city. This symphony is a tone-painting of life in London.

At first the listener finds himself on the bank of the "calm and silent Thames." This theme, which recurs constantly, is the mysterious voice of the river.

Presently, above the silence, come the chimes of the famous clock "Big Ben" striking the half hour. (This passage is played by the harp.)

The listener, turning from the river, now makes his way into the crowded streets, swarming with people, raucous with whistles and shouts. And now he turns again out of the turmoil and goes back through various districts to the river. From the opposite bank rise the Saturday night sounds of the slums, overborne later by the "Hunger March" of the unemployed, pinched with cold, starving. And then again silence as in the beginning, with only the sluggish voice of the Thames, and Big Ben sounding from Westminster Tower.

You will notice in this the two characteristics which we have already pointed out as belonging to modern compositions —nationality and a strong leaning toward programme music. The symphony paints scenes, and those scenes are taken from the very soul of English metropolitan life. By creating that work, Vaughn Williams has definitely taken a place among the foremost musicians of England.

Granville Bantock, Eugene Goosens and Frank Bridge are among the present day English composers. John Ireland, too, is of that group and he, perhaps, shows the most sincerity. Though in some respects he reflects the style of Debussy, he yet has many original touches.

It seems only a step from the consideration of English composers to the study of our own American music. But in the few brief centuries since the settlement of this country, our musical history has been changed by so many circumstances peculiar to the New World, that we shall find the development of American music a very distinct study by itself. How the instinct for music, in spite of discouragements, took root here in New England and later spread throughout the country, we shall study in the next and final chapter of this course.

The following phonograph records may be used to illustrate some of the musical selections in this chapter.

Title	Victor Record No.
CHILDREN'S CORNER SUITE (*Debussy*).	7147-7148
SONGS MY MOTHER TAUGHT ME from *Gypsy Songs* (Dvořák) Ponselle.	1319
NEW WORLD SYMPHONY—(Dvořák)—Philadelphia Orchestra.	6565-6569
POMP AND CIRCUMSTANCE (Elgar)—Chicago Orchestra and Organ.	6648
PEER GYNT SUITE (Grieg)—Victor Symphony Orchestra. Part I and II.	35793
Part III and IV.	20245
CONCERTO IN A MINOR (Grieg)—De Greef and Royal Albert Hall Orchestra.	9151-9154
BOLERO (Ravel)—Boston Symphony Orchestra.	7251-7252
MOLLY ON THE SHORE (Grainger) — Philadelphia String Simfonietta.	11560
SONG OF THE FLEA (Moussorgsky)—Chaliapin.	6783
VISSI D' ARTE from *Tosca* (Puccini)—Jeritza.	1346
Fantasie from *Madame Butterfly* (Puccini)—Victor Symphony Orchestra.	35786
MY NAME IS MIMI from *La Bohème* (Puccini)—Bori.	6790
MELODY IN *F* (Rubinstein)—Casals (Cello).	1178
SUITE ALGÉRIENNE (Saint-Saëns)—Continental Symphony Orchestra.	9296
THE SWAN (Saint-Saëns)—Casals (Cello).	1143
THE MIKADO—Selections (Sullivan)—Victor Light Opera Company.	35796
QUARTET FROM RIGOLETTO (Verdi)—Galli-Curci, Homer, Gigli, and de Luca.	10012

Title	Victor Record No.
SONG OF THE VOLGA BOATMEN (Russian Folksong)—Chaliapin.	6822
PACIFIC 231 (Honegger)—Continental Symphony Orchestra.	9276
LOVE FOR THREE ORANGES (Prokofieff)—London Symphony Orchestra.	9128
PETROUCHKA SUITE (Stravinsky)—Boston Symphony Orchestra.	6998-7000
APOLLON MUSAGETE (Stravinsky)—Boston Symphony Orchestra.	7000
FIRE BIRD (Stravinsky)—Philadelphia Symphony Orchestra.	6773-6775
SONG OF THE VIKING GUEST FROM SADKO (Rimsky-Korsakoff) Chaliapin.	6867
FLIGHT OF A BUMBLE BEE FROM CZAR SULTAN (Rimsky-Korsakoff)—Chicago Symphony Orchestra.	6579
POLOVETZKI DANCE FROM PRINCE IGOR (Borodin)—Philadelphia Symphony Orchestra.	6514
ORIENTALE (Cui)—Elman.	1354
DANSE ORIENTALE (Glazounov)—Philadelphia Symphony Orchestra.	1335
FOUNTAINS OF ROME (Respighi)—London Symphony Orchestra.	9126-9127
WALTZ (Ravel) Coates—Symphony Orchestra.	9130-9131
ISLAMEY (Balakirev)—Hollywood Bowl Orchestra.	6870
ROUET D'OMPHALE (Saint-Saëns)—New York Philharmonic Symphony Orchestra.	7006
DON JUAN (Strauss) Coates—Symphony Orchestra.	9114-9115
SYMPHONY IN D MINOR (Franck)—Philadelphia Symphony Orchestra.	6726-6730
AFTERNOON OF A FAUN (Debussy)—Philadelphia Symphony Orchestra.	6696
SYMPHONY No. 1, C MINOR (Brahms)—Philadelphia Symphony.	6657-6662
I ATTEMPT FROM LOVE'S SICKNESS TO FLY (Purcell)—Dadmun.	4009
SYMPHONY B MINOR (Pathétique) (Tchaikovsky) Boston Symphony Orchestra.	7294-7298
PICTURES AT AN EXPOSITION (Moussorgsky-Ravel)—Boston Symphony Orchestra.	7372-7375
SCHEHERAZADE SUITE (Rimsky-Korsakov)—Philadelphia Symphony Orchestra.	6738-6742

Title	Victor Record No.
CLASSICAL SYMPHONY (Prokofieff)—Boston Symphony Orchestra.	7196-7197
DON QUIXOTE (Strauss)—New York Philharmonic Orchestra (Sir Thomas Beecham conducting)	7589-7593
LE TOMBEAU DE COUPERIN (Ravel)—Société des Concerts du Conservatoire	11150-11151
POEM OF ECSTASY (Scriabin)—Philadelphia Symphony Orchestra.	7515-7518
DAPHNIS ET CHLOE (Ravel)—Boston Symphony Orchestra.	7143-7144
WIEGENLIED (Brahms)—Lashanska.	7085
WALTZES (Brahms)—Bachaus.	7990
HUNGARIAN DANCES (Brahms)—British Broadcasting Company Symphony Orchestra.	11534
SYMPHONY No. 4, A MINOR (Sibelius).	7683-7686

OUTSTANDING RECENT RECORDINGS
Suggested for College and University Libraries
ANCIENT INSTRUMENTS, AMERICAN SOCIETY OF THE

	Victor Record No.
CHIMENE (Sacchini, 1734-1788), DIVERTISSEMENT (Jean Joseph Mouret, 1682-1738)—American Society of the Ancient Instruments, Ben Stad, Director.	1635
1. PAVANE, 2. GALLIARD (William Byrd, 1542-1623), CHACONNE (Henry Purcell, 1658-1695)—American Society of the Ancient Instruments, Ben Stad, Director.	7873

BACH, JOHANN SEBASTIAN

	Victor Record No.
BRANDENBURG CONCERTO No. 5, IN D MAJOR—Cortot, Thibaud, Cortet and École Normale Chamber Orchestra.	7863, 7864
BRANDENBURG CONCERTO No. 6 IN Bb—École Normale Chamber Orchestra.	11264, 11265
CONCERTO FOR TWO VIOLINS IN D MINOR—Yehudi Menuhin, Georges Enesco and Orchestra, cond. by Pierre Monteux.	7732, 7733
SONATA IN C MAJOR (Unaccompanied)—Yehudi Menuhin.	Album M-148 (7615 to 7617)
SONATA IN D MINOR (Unaccompanied)—Adolf Busch.	Album M-133 (7554 to 7556)
SUITE IN G (Bach-Goossens) — Courante, Allemande, Bourrée, Gavotte, Menuet, Gigue — London Symphony Orchestra, conducted by Eugene Goossens.	11427

BEETHOVEN, LUDWIG VAN

CONCERTO IN E FLAT (The Emperor) — Artur Schnabel —
London Symphony Orch., cond. by Dr. Malcom Sargent. Album M-155
(7639 to 7643)

CONCERTO No. 1 IN C MAJOR—Artur Schnabel, London Symphony Orchestra, conducted by Dr. Malcolm Sargent. Album M-158
(7669 to 7673)

CONCERTO No. 4 IN G MAJOR—Artur Schnabel, London Philharmonic Orchestra, conducted by Dr. Malcolm Sargent. Album M-156
(7661 to 7664)

QUARTET IN B FLAT MAJOR—Budapest String Quartet. Album M-157
(11409 to 11412)

SYMPHONY No. 8 IN F MAJOR—British Broadcasting Company
Symphony Orchestra, conducted by Adrian Boult. Album M-181
(11535 to 11537)

BIZET—DI CAPUA—VERDI

O SOLE MIO (di Capua), RIGOLETTO—LA DONNA E MOBILE
(Woman is Fickle) (Verdi)—Enrico Caruso. 1616

AIDA—CELESTE AIDA (Verdi), PEARL FISHERS—JE CROIS EN-
TENDRE ENCORE (Bizet)—Enrico Caruso. 7770

BLOCH, ERNEST

QUINTET FOR PIANO AND STRINGS—Alfredo Casella, Pro Arte
Quartet. Album M-191
(7874 to 7877)

BRAHMS, JOHANNES

BRAHMS LIEDER—Rose Bampton, Conrad Thibault. Album M-175
(1610, 1611, 7759, 7760, 7761)

DIE MAINACHT, also SELIGKEIT (Schubert), RASTLOSE LIEBE
(Schubert)—Ria Ginster. 7821

NACHTIGALL (The Nightingale), STÄNDCHEN (Serenade), FEL-
DEINSAMKEIT (In Summer Fields)—Elena Gerhardt. 7793

VERGEBLICHES STÄNDCHEN (The Vain Suit), DAS MÄDCHEN
SPRICHT (The Maiden Speaks), AUF DEM KIRCHHOFE (In the
Church Yard)—Elena Gerhardt. 7794

WIE KOMM' ICH DENN ZUR TÜR HEREIN (And If I come unto
your Door), MEIN MÄDEL HAT 'NEN ROSENMUND (My
Maiden hath a mouth of Red), FEINSLIEBCHEN, DU SOLLST
MIR NICHT BARFUSS' GEH'N (My Darling shall never with bare
feet go), ERLAUBE MIR, FEINSLIEBCHEN (Allow me) — Elena
Gerhardt. 7795

QUARTET IN B FLAT MAJOR—Budapest String Quartet.   Album M-183
(11545 to 11548)

QUINTET IN G MAJOR, OPUS 111—Budapest String Quartet, 2nd
Viola, Hans Mahlke.   Album M-184
(11553 to 11555)

SERENADE—SCHERZO AND MINUET—Leo Blech, London Symphony Orchestra.   11458

SYMPHONY No. 4 IN E MINOR—Leopold Stokowski, Philadelphia Orchestra.   Album M-185
(7825 and 7829)

TRAGIC OVERTURE, HUNGARIAN DANCES—British Broadcasting
Company Orchestra, conducted by Adrian Boult.   11533 and 11534

BYRD, WILLIAM

(See Ancient Instruments)

CARPENTER, JOHN ALDEN

WHEN I BRING TO YOU COLOUR'D TOYS (Tagore—Carpenter),
LIGHT, MY LIGHT (Tagore—Carpenter)—Rose Bampton.   1628

CHOPIN, FREDERIC FRANÇOIS

SCHERZO No. 1, B MINOR—SCHERZO No. 2, B♭—SCHERZO No.
3, C SHARP MINOR—SCHERZO No. 4, E MAJOR—Arthur
Rubinstein.   Album M-189
(7855 to 7858)

DEBUSSY, CLAUDE ACHILLE

QUARTET FOR STRINGS IN G MINOR—Pro Arte Quartet.   Album M-186
(7835 to 7838)

RHAPSODY FOR SAXOPHONE — Symphony Orchestra, conducted
by P. Coppola, Saxophone Solo, M. Viard.   11426

RHAPSODY FOR CLARINET—Symphony Orchestra, conducted by
Piero Coppola, Clarinet Solo, Gaston Hamelin.   11433

D'INDY, VINCENT

ISTAR SYMPHONIC VARIATIONS, PARTS 1 AND 2—Orchestra of
Paris Conservatory, conducted by Piero Coppola.   11559

ISTAR, PART III, MOLLY ON THE SHORE (Grainger)—Philadelphia String Simfonietta, conducted by Fabien Sevitzky.   11560

ELGAR, EDWARD WILLIAM

CONCERTO IN B MINOR—Yehudi Menuhin, London Symphony
Orchestra, conducted by Sir Edward Elgar.   Album M-174
(7747 to 7752)

GLINKA, MICHAEL IVANOVICH

RUSSLAN AND LUDMILLA — Rond of Farlaf, ROUSSALKA — Aria
of the Miller (Dargomwizhsky)—Feodor Chaliapin.   7704

GOOSENS, EUGENE
(See Bach)

GRAINGER, PERCY ALDRIDGE
(See d'Indy)

GRETCHANINOFF, ALEXANDER

CREDO, The Creed (Archangelsky)—Chaliapin with Choir of
Russian Metro. Church.   7715

HAYDN, FRANZ JOSEF

SYMPHONY IN C MAJOR (Salomon Set)—London Symphony
Orchestra, conducted by Hans Weisbach.   Album M-140
(11317 to 11319)

LITURGICAL MUSIC

LITURGICAL MUSIC OF THE CATHOLIC CHURCH—Choir of the
Sistine Chapel of Rome, conducted by Mgr. Rella.   Album M-182
(7811 to 7814)

MOUSSORGSKY, MODESTE

GOPAK—"The Fair At Sorotchinsk," CORTEGE DES NOBLES
(Mlada) (Rimsky-Korsakow)—Albert Coates, London Symphony Orchestra.   11443

NIGHT ON BARE MOUNTAIN—Albert Coates, London Symphony
Orchestra.   11448

MOURET, JEAN JOSEPH
(See Ancient Instruments)

MOZART, WOLFGANG

SONATA IN A MAJOR—Jose Iturbi.   11593 and 11594

DIE ENTFÜHRUNG AUS DEM SERAIL — MARTEN ALLER ARTEN
(Thou may'st learn to hate Me), LE NOZZE DI FIGARO—VOI
CHE SAPETE (Tell me, Ladies, You who know)—Ria Ginster.   7822

LES PETITS RIENS — Ballet Music — Overture, Gavotte, Panto-
mine, Gavotte—Blech, London Symphony Orchestra.   11445

PROKOFIEFF, SERGE

CONCERTO NO. 3 IN C MAJOR — Prokofieff, London Symphony
Orchestra, conducted by Piero Coppola.   Album M-176
(7772 to 7774)

LE PAS D'ACIER—Coates, London Symphony Orchestra.   11446 and 11447

PURCELL, HENRY

(See Ancient Instruments)

RAVEL, MAURICE

TZIGANE—Yehudi Menuhin.   7810

RIMSKY-KORSAKOFF, NICHOLAS A.

MAY NIGHT—Overture—Albert Coates, London Symphony Orch.   11424

SNOW MAIDEN—Dance of the Tumblers, IVAN THE TERRIBLE—
Storm Music—Coates, London Symphony Orchestra.   11454

ROSSINI, GIOACCHINO

BARBIERE DI SEVIGLIA—UNA VOCE POCO FA (A little Voice I
hear), RIGOLETTO—CARO NOME (Dearest Name)—Tettraz-
zini, orchestra conducted by Lawrence Collingwood.   7883

SACCHINI, ANTONIO GASPARO

(See Ancient Instruments)

SCHUBERT, FRANZ PETER

AVE MARIA — DU BIST DIE RUH' (My Sweet repose) — Mme.
Hulda Lashanska.   7778

RASTLOSE LIEBE (Restless love), SELIGKEIT (Happiness)—Ria
Ginster.   7821

SCHUMANN, ROBERT

SCENES OF CHILDHOOD—Benno Moiséivitch.   7705 and 7706

MODERN SPANISH MUSIC

MODERN SPANISH MUSIC—George Copeland.   Album M-178
(1623, 1624, 7781, 7782)

STRAUSS, RICHARD

WALTZ FROM "INTERMEZZO" — Karl Alwin, Vienna Philharmonic Orchestra.   11430

SZOSTAKOWICZ, A.

SYMPHONY NO. 1, OPUS 10—Stokowski, Philadelphia Orch.   Album M-192
(7884 to 7888)

TCHAIKOVSKY, PETER ILYITCH

CONCERTO NO. 1 IN Bb MINOR — Arthur Rubinstein, London
Symphony Orchestra, conducted by John Barbirolli.   Album M-180
(7802 to 7805)

SYMPHONY NO. 3 IN D MAJOR — Albert Coates, London Symphony Orchestra.   Album M-166
(11459 to 11462)

VERDI, GUISEPPE

OTELLO (Complete) — Soloists, Chorus, and Orchestra of La
Scala, conducted by Carlo Sabajno.   Album M-152
(11363 to 11378)

(See also Bizet)

VIVALDI, ANTONIO

CONCERTO IN G MINOR (Vivadli-Nachez) — Mischa Elman,
London Symph. Orch., cond. by Lawrence Collingwood.   7585 and 7586

WAGNER, RICHARD

DIE FEEN—Overture—Albert Coates, London Symphony Orch.   11455

GÖTTERDÄMMERUNG (Excerpts)—Stokowski, Philadelphia Orchestra, assisted by Agnes Davis.   Album M-188
(7843 to 7847)

MEISTERSINGER — GUT'N ABEND, MEISTERS! (Good Evening,
Masters), MEISTERSINGER— ICH SEH' 'SWAR NUR (I see why
'twas) — Friedrich Schorr, Göta Ljüngberg, London Symphony Orchestra.   7680

DAS RHEINGOLD (Wagner-Stokowski)—Stokowski, Philadelphia
Orchestra.   Album M-179
(7796 to 7798)

SIEGFRIED (Finale of Act III) — Lauritz Melchior, Florence
Easton, Royal Opera Orchestra, cond. by Robert Heger.   Album M-167
(7762 to 7765)

VON WEBER, CARL MARIA

PETER SCHMOLL — Overture—Vienna Philharmonic Orchestra,
conducted by Clemens Kraus.   11429

QUESTIONS

1. Name the two basic principles which have strongly influenced most modern music. From what you have studied in this chapter, do you suppose that general interest in folksongs has increased or diminished during the past century?

2. Tell what you know about the musical style of Debussy.

3. Discuss briefly the present state of music in England.

4. What peoples have recently developed their characteristic national music? Name five composers who have taken a keen interest in building up *national* music.

5. Tell your own impressions of the Grieg *Folksong* selection quoted in this chapter.

6. Give a full explanation of key relationship. Find the attendant keys of the following scales: Re (D), Sol (G), La (A) major; si (b) and re (d) minor.

7. State the characteristics of a composition written with regard to (1) tonality, (2) polytonality, and (3) atonality.

8. What is the difference between metrical and rhythmical music?

Chapter X

AMERICAN MUSIC

To study the history of the development of music in America one should begin with the music of the Aborigines, the first music of all that can be traced on this continent. We find, however, that the music of these North American Indians has had very little, if any, influence on our music of later times, and also their music is not of a sort to be broadly appreciated by those whom we call "American" today. To be sure Indian music is not without its interest for us, and we shall discuss it later in this chapter; but for the present we must set it aside while we search for the origins of that music which is American in the same sense that we are American.

American music of that sort, we find, began in "the rigid, narrow and often commonplace psalm-singing of New England." Although there were civilized people in America for almost a generation before the Puritans and Pilgrims, the English colonists in Virginia adhered strictly to the songs which they brought with them from England, and made no attempt to develop songs better fitted to the spirit of their new surroundings, nor any attempt to establish schools of music. Their music was purely English in feeling and not American.

The music that developed in Puritan Boston and Pilgrim Plymouth was far less artistic, and though it had its origin overseas, it soon became closely associated with the Massachusetts Bay settlements. At the very start both Pilgrims and Puritans united in distrusting music! They would have abolished it all but for the fact that the Hebrews, who served to some extent as a pattern for the Puritan form of worship, had undoubtedly employed psalm-singing in their religious services. Therefore the Puritans had the psalms sung during their own services, and it is recorded that at first only five or six tunes were used, probably *Old Hundred, York, Hackney, St. Mary's Tune, Windsor* and *Martyrs*. These tunes served for public worship in Plymouth for seventy years and in Salem for forty.

128

The version of the Psalms used for singing was that which had been prepared for the Pilgrims in Amsterdam by one of their pastors, Henry Ainsworth, but in Boston this was soon superseded by the *Bay Psalm Book* published in Cambridge, Massachusetts, in 1640. With the exception of a trivial almanac, this was the first book printed in the Colonies.

Hymns—that is, church songs based on words not taken from the Book of Psalms—were not as yet admitted into either Pilgrim or Puritan services, but a few appeared in the *Bay Psalm Book*. This most widely used Psalm book contained no music until the ninth edition, printed in 1698, included thirteen tunes in two-part harmony. The custom of "lining-out" the hymns was resorted to because of the scarcity of books. The "lining-out" was performed by the minister or the deacon, who read line by line the text that was to be sung, the congregation pausing in their singing at the end of each phrase sufficiently long to allow this piece-meal recitation. The result of this was sometimes a most awkward one, when the necessary pause at the end of a line disturbed or even contradicted the sense of the poem, as in the following quotation:

"The Lord will come, and He will not"

and in the next line,

"Keep silence, but speak out."

Fortunately, even when musical matters were at the lowest ebb, there were some cultured men among the clergy who worked hard to build up a better school of singing in church service. Mather, Symmes, Walter, Prince and others labored hard to elevate this part of the Puritan education. But there was strong opposition whenever any special attention was paid to the music; and singing by note, or anything that savored of skill in music, was regarded as decidedly heterodox. Many went so far as to consider skillful singing a direct sin. Nevertheless, out of the desire to sing the psalms properly there came the earliest New England singing schools. One existed in Boston as early as 1717, and about this time we find published a number of psalm-books, which were, in fact, primitive vocal methods. Nothing difficult was attempted; no use was made of a fine harmonization like that of Ravenscroft; all that the methods explained was how to sing simple melodies by note. Singing by note was called the "new way," and of the many who were naturally opposed to it, one gave his views on the subject as follows (this was in 1723):

"Truly I have a great jealousy that if we once begin to sing by rule, the next thing will be to pray by rule, and preach by rule; and then comes popery."

From the singing-schools there gradually and unconsciously began choir-singing. This was a natural course, since those attending the schools advanced more musically than those who did not. And the musical ones started having special meetings so that they could sing the psalms together, thereby making a great improvement in the singing during the services. These special singers were soon assigned special seats, and came to be regarded as a separate body of worshippers—the choir.

Because of the victory of the singing-schools and choirs in the last half of the eighteenth century, books of music began to follow each other in profusion. It was about this time that some few suggested using an organ in the divine service as was the custom in foreign countries, but this proposition brought a conflict of opinions which lasted a full century.

As early as 1713 Mr. Brattle, a Puritan of Boston, but very liberal and fond of art, gave by will an organ to the Brattle Square Church. But that church was not yet ready to receive such an instrument into its services, so the unwelcome gift was handed on to King's Chapel, Boston, where it was used for years. This was the first pipe-organ set up in a New England church, and its first organist had to be brought over from England on purpose to play it.

By 1798 we find secular music had been fairly well established, and several books containing a collection of the newest and most celebrated "Sentimental, Convivial, Humorous, Hunting, Sea and Masonic Songs" were published. As early as 1756 a Concert Hall was built in Boston where many entertainments and concerts of secular music were given. There was dancing after the concerts as a rule. Josiah Flagg established a band in 1773, became its leader, and gave concerts in Faneuil Hall and elsewhere, directing on one occasion as many as fifty musicians.

The first American poet-composer was Francis Hopkinson. He was born in Philadelphia, September 21, 1737, and was a graduate of the first class to receive degrees from the College of Philadelphia, and one of the most prominent patriots of the Revolutionary War. As a member of the Continental Congress he signed the Declaration of Independence. All through the Revolutionary War he was constantly writing prose and verse, mostly of a satirical character, in support of his political faith. The most famous of these was *The Battle of Keys*, written in 1778.

Hopkinson began the study of harpsichord at the age of seventeen. Later he became an accomplished organ player. He composed many songs, the most important volume being called: *Seven Songs for Harpsichord and Forte Piano.* He added an eighth song after the cover had been engraved, and we find this advertisement: *A Set of Eight Songs,—Words and Music composed by Francis Hopkinson.* These songs are composed in an easy, familiar style, intended for young "practitioners" on the Harpsichord or Forte Piano, and is the first work of this kind attempted in the United States. This book was published in Philadelphia, November, 1788. Hopkinson died May 9, 1791.

FRANCIS HOPKINSON
(1737-1791)

Mr. Sonneck in his book on *Francis Hopkinson and James Lyon* states that Francis Hopkinson's song *My Days Have Been So Wondrous Free* is the earliest secular American composition in existence. It was written in 1759. The original composition is given below.

My Days Have Been So Wondrous Free

FRANCIS HOPKINSON
(1737-1791)

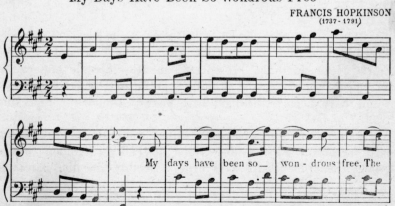

To William Billings, who was born in Boston, October 7, 1746, and who died there September 28, 1800, many historians give the credit for being the first American composer. He was a tanner by trade, and it is said he chalked down his earliest compositions upon sides of leather. His musical education was limited probably to the singing schools (for he was a choir singer as well as a composer), but this in no way dismayed him, for he believed that natural taste would guide the true musician in composition, without the necessity of studying rules. He was an eccentric and uncouth character, a fair butt for the ridicule which many of his fellow citizens flung at him, but his earnestness and sincerity in all he did and his great patriotism won him a favorable standing with some influential people. He was a believer in the effects of florid counterpoint (of its rules he was ignorant), and he early began to introduce in his works "fugue-tunes," such fugueing (as one historian describes it) "as might make Bach's bones rattle!"

But for all the criticism Billings received, his music deserved to be saved from oblivion; it was melodic and cheerful and strongly rhythmic. It cheered many a fireside and camp, for it was not above the popular intelligence, when higher art would have been. Billings' best known composition was the hymn *Chester*.

Later came a succession of other composers of whom the most important were Andrew Law and Oliver Holden, whose hymn *Coronation* is still a favorite. By this time the character of the Puritan Church showed a tendency to relax; yet it was still necessary to cloak innocent amusement under the garb of religion, and the study of music was still held to be a dubious proceeding unless it were sanctified by being devoted to religious ends. We find, towards the end of the eighteenth century, that plays were occasionally smuggled into popular acceptance under the title of *Moral Lectures*. But the "ice" was gradually breaking, and the beginning of the nineteenth century found matters free for the advance of American music.

The music of New England has been spoken of first because this was the seed from which grew the earliest American school of composition. In Philadelphia during the latter part of the eighteenth century we find the art-centre of America. Its culture was almost European in advancement. The first really ambitious concert took place in Philadelphia in 1786.

The chief music of New York was found in the Episcopal churches. Trinity Church upheld something of the dignity of the English cathedral music within its walls. Outside the churches the public did not desire classical music of any kind, and the few musical societies that were founded in the eighteenth century soon died from lack of appreciation. Baltimore, New Orleans, and Charleston, S. C. possessed some musical activities but nothing that influenced the progress of American music.

People began presently to realize that a musical atmosphere is essential to musical development and progress, and that such an atmosphere comes only from *organized* effort in musical work. Consequently, we find being established various musical societies, whose work in performing the best works of the day (oratorios, and the like) was one of the most important steps in enlightening the people as a whole. The first of these was the Stoughton (Mass.) Musical Society, which grew out of a singing class formed in 1774 by Billings. The most famous and most significant of the older musical bodies, however, was the Handel and Haydn Society, still in existence, which was organized in Boston in 1815, with a chorus of nearly one hundred voices. Boston had at that time a number of well-trained musicians, and others came there from Europe in later years, making the city for a long time the centre of American musical life.

In 1826 Lowell Mason, then about thirty-five years old,

came to Boston to begin a musical career which formed a link between the early singing school and the work of the present day. He was essentially a man of the people among whom he lived, and by nature was an efficient teacher. He traveled over New England and parts of New York State, holding musical conventions, and teaching the principles of music to hundreds of singers and teachers from far and near. His great work thus closely touched the people; and in a day when music was not taught in the public schools, he contributed more than one can now believe to spread a love for and a knowledge of vocal music. He died in 1872.

The growth of interest in music arising from the choral societies, the labors of Lowell Mason, and the art of foreign musicians who came to this country created a demand for music, other than vocal and organ, for many of the foreigners especially had played in orchestras in Europe. As early as 1796 there was formed in Boston an orchestra called the "Philharmonic Society," directed by the able pioneer Gottlieb Graupner. This was the first permanent orchestra. Then in 1848 another important one was organized by some young Europeans, in New York, and called the "Germania Orchestra." This latter orchestra may be called the first organization to give satisfactory performances of the great symphonies in America.

In 1833 came the next important advance in music when Lowell Mason and others founded in Boston the Academy of Music. This was primarily a conservatory of music; yet its activities also included the presentation of lectures and concerts of a high order, the publication of essays, and a determined effort to raise the standard of music in the school and in the church. It formed an orchestra, and for a time was considered the leading American authority on orchestral music. But the Academy's greatest achievement was in promoting the development of public school music. The planting of that seed has since proved one of the greatest factors in the musical advancement of America.

In 1837 the Harvard Musical Association came into existence and from that time on exerted a strong and active influence on the music not alone in Boston but of other cities as well. Much of its effort was bent toward bringing to the people the best music that had been written. That meant first of all the building up of musical organizations that could perform such music. To that end a Harvard Musical Association orchestra was formed, which in 1866 gave symphonic concerts in Boston. But even before that time the Association had arranged a series of concerts devoted to "chamber music,"—that is, instrumental works for string quartets, quintets or similar groups, usually composed in the sonata form. In the field of vocal music, the Association lent its influence by giving Glee Club concerts; and by founding a musical library it greatly encouraged the wider study of music. It was the Harvard Musical Association, too, which agitated the subject of a music hall for Boston, with the result that one was opened in 1852.

BOSTON SYMPHONY ORCHESTRA

The credit for raising the standard of orchestral performance and for helping the public generally to appreciate music of the classic school belongs first of all to Theodore Thomas (1835-1905). His earliest efforts had as their aim the better and wider performance of chamber music in this country. His interest soon extended, however, to the larger orchestral forms. With the help of Dr. William Mason, son of the celebrated

Lowell Mason, he arranged various concerts and traveled from city to city with an orchestra of remarkably fine ability. One significant result of this work was the stimulation of musical pride in Boston and the founding of the Boston Symphony Orchestra. Mr. William Arms Fisher, in his *Notes On Music In Old Boston*, says: "The frequent visits of his [Thomas'] orchestra to Boston overshadowed the less disciplined and imperfect local body, sharpened musical perception, and wakened concert-goers to the need of an orchestra of like technical refinement and masterly leadership. This need was generously met by Mr. Henry Lee Higginson when he founded the Boston Symphony Orchestra, which gave its first concert under Georg Henschel, October 22, 1881, and under Gericke, Nikisch, and their successors, has developed into the present unique organization." The brilliance of this orchestra has done much to stimulate musical interest throughout the country; and there have since been developed orchestras of high rank in Chicago in 1891 as a direct result of Thomas' activity; Cincinnati in 1895; Philadelphia in 1900; St. Louis in 1907; San Francisco in 1909; Detroit in 1914; and Cleveland in 1918; not to mention other less known organizations. The oldest orchestral body in continuous service is the Philharmonic Society of New York organized in 1842. It was under the able leadership of Theodore Thomas for twelve years before he went to Chicago, and under him and his notable successor, Anton Seidl, it reached its zenith.

It is difficult to find any music which is characteristically American. There is music characteristic of American types, such as that of the American negro and of the American Indian, but of music which bears the stamp of the American Nation and all its types there is very little—some say none. This is not unnatural since we are such a young country and a country made up of so many nationalities. Good music is a natural growth out of the past and America has very little musical past. Europe has had good music for so many centuries that every individual has a background upon which to work; America, on the other hand, is still creating her own background.

Henry Gilbert, probably more than any other, has contributed to that background. He at first thought our music should be based on Indian or Negro music, but later he grew to feel that American music should comprehend something more, and has gone far toward developing Americanism in music.

The American composer who has achieved the most far-reaching reputation for originality is Edward A. MacDowell (1861-1908). That MacDowell's talent survived even the pedantry of German conservatories is the strongest proof of its innate and incorrigible originality. He was a poet, nature-worshipper, and romanticist who dwelt in a realm of his own outside the confines of the period or community. He spent a great part of his time in Peterboro, New Hampshire, where he lived in his log-cabin and did much of his best composing. He would not cut down a tree for he was certain that the spirit which it harbored suffered from the axe. His nature ex-

MACDOWELL (1861-1908)

pressed itself characteristically in short but exquisite melodies, of which the following is a famous example.

From an Indian Lodge *

EDWARD A. MacDOWELL, Op. 51, № 5

His music is very individual, like no one else's but MacDowell's. Though he is most generally known by such simple

---

*See *Woodland Sketches, Op. 51,* By Edward A. MacDowell; published by Arthur P. Schmidt. Used by permission.

tunes as the above, the richness and depth of his talent are most fully shown in such compositions as the *Celtic Sonata*. In 1896 he accepted the position of Professor of Music in Columbia University in New York City and held this position until

INDIAN CHIEF, SHORT BULL

1904, when he resigned. It is thought the strain of his life connected with the University helped to bring on nervousness. He was not a man for an academic life. His creative activities were necessarily circumscribed. These conditions and increased nervous strain hastened his unhappy end. He died in 1908, and American music was bereaved.

Among the present day composers there are several whose lives and achievements are worth careful study. Since, however, there is no room in a course of this length to discuss any one composer fully, we shall give only a brief paragraph to each. If you are interested in learning more about the members of this modern group, you can easily find in the libraries both biographies and collections of their finest works.

One of the most distinguished American composers was George W. Chadwick (1854-1931), who probably did more than

A Ballad of Trees and the Master

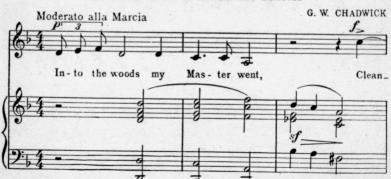

Moderato alla Marcia

G. W. CHADWICK

In-to the woods my Mas-ter went, Clean—

for- spent, In - to the woods my Mas-ter came, For-

spent with love and shame.

Copyright MDCCCXCIX by Oliver Ditson Company

But the o - lives they were not

blind to Him, The lit - tle grey leaves were

kind to Him: The thorn - - tree had a

mind to Him When in- to the woods He__ came.

any other American but MacDowell to give status and repute to
native composers.   He was head of the New England Conservatory
of Music from 1897 until his death in 1931.   He was the most
productive of American musicians and one of the most fertile in
melodic invention and technical device.   As a teacher his influence was far-reaching.   His versatility is shown in the wide
field covered by his compositions, which include works in practically all of the principal forms.   His choral and orchestral works
especially have won praise.

Horatio Parker (1863-1919), a pupil of Chadwick's and
later of European teachers, is the composer of what in the opinion
of many is the most beautiful sacred choral work which has come
from America—*Hora Novissima*, composed in 1893 and performed repeatedly with great success both in England and America.   He is also the composer of the operas *Mona* and *Fairyland*.

Arthur Foote (1853-   ), who was one of Paine's most
noted pupils and who gained his musical education entirely in

America, is another composer and teacher whose influence on American music has been marked. Certain of his songs, piano pieces, organ works and chamber-music have gone far and wide.

Edgar Stillman Kelley (1857-   ) studied under various teachers in this country and at the Stuttgart Conservatory. His high technical equipment, his mastery of the orchestra is more than matched by the poetic and dramatic power of his inspiration. His incidental music to *Ben Hur*, his *Aladdin Suite* and *Alice in Wonderland Suite* for orchestra, his *New England Symphony* and more than all his musical Mystery Play *Pilgrim's Progress* have won him a high place among contemporary composers both in America and Europe.

Frederick S. Converse (1871-   ) also studied with Paine. He is a composer of the highest ideals. His *Mystic Trumpeter* is considered one of the finest of American tone-poems for orchestra. His works include two operas, *The Pipe of Desire* and *The Sacrifice*, a symphony, an oratorio and numerous songs and violin numbers. His *Elegiac Poem* makes use of some negro melodies, but his *Flivver Ten Million* is the most American of his compositions.

John Alden Carpenter is one of our best composers. He has tried to interpret the most familiar phases of our everyday life. Among his orchestral compositions are *Adventures in a Perambulator*, *Krazy Kat* and *Skyscrapers*.

Deems Taylor recently wrote the score to an American opera called *The King's Henchman*, text written by Edna St. Vincent Millay. Though written by Americans, the opera is hardly typically American. More characteristic in subject matter is Cadman's opera *The Witch of Salem*. An interesting development in the production of Opera in America was made by the "American Opera Company," which produced opera in English. They gave fresh interpretations to the operas, untrammeled by convention and having regard for the full meaning of the opera both dramatically and musically.

Among our younger composers Aaron Copland shows genuine ability. His concerto for piano and orchestra is remarkable for its rhythms. He has many musical ideas.

Recently a prize was offered by *Musical America* for the best American composition by an American composer. It was won by

Bloch, a Swiss who came to this country in 1912. He called his composition *America,* an epic Symphony, in which he traced the history of America from the sailing of the Pilgrims from England up to the present day.

Edward Burlingame Hill, Rubin Goldmark and John Powell are other serious American composers. The two last have each written a *Negro Rhapsody* in which they use the beautiful themes and rhythms of the negro folkmusic.

To the names of these men should be added that of Mrs. H. H. A. Beach, one of the few women composers to have written with distinction in the higher forms of music, as for example her *Gaelic Symphony* and various compositions of chamber-music. Her songs and piano pieces are widely known.

We have learned how the *folksongs* of each country by their peculiarities of rhythm, form, and melody have reflected the national spirit of the people who created them. And we have seen how skilful composers have availed themselves of "the song of the people" as a foundation or inspiration for many of their compositions. It is those countries where music, however simple, has been a part of the every day life for a great majority of the people, an inheritance which has come to them with their national traits and characteristics, where it is a means of expression for a feeling or emotion more strongly marked than ordinary—it is those countries that have produced the greatest musical minds. In such lands the composer has become in a way an interpreter of the feelings of his countrymen and has voiced the unexpressed emotions and impulses of many generations.

Bearing all this in mind, we are naturally led to ask, has America also a folksong? The answer is, America is handicapped in the production of folksong both by its business activity and by the fact that it is a gathering of many nations who are not yet welded together into a *distinct* type; but in the South, which possesses in its negro population a well distinguished race of natural singers, we find music which is practically folksong, remarkably different from the music of any other nations.

It has been objected that this music of the negroes is not American, but really African in part. Yet we may be sure that if the negroes had remained in Africa they would not have pro-

duced this music; it is a product of the negro as he is influenced
by American surroundings and by life on the plantations.

The folksongs of the plantation show melody, direct emotion, and a harmony that is simple but effective. The "spiritual"
or religious songs predominate. The reason for this readily is
found; slavery was the sorrow of the Southern blacks; religion
was their comfort and refuge. Booker T. Washington bears
this testimony: "The negro folksong has for the negro race the
same value that the folksong of any other people has for that
people. It reminds the race of the 'rock whence it was hewn,'
it fosters race pride; and in the days of slavery it furnished an
outlet for the anguish of smitten hearts. The plantation songs
known as the 'spirituals' are the spontaneous outbursts of intense
religious fervor, and had their origin chiefly in the camp-meetings,
the revivals and in other religious exercises. They breathe a
childlike faith in a personal Father and glow with the hope that
the children of bondage will ultimately pass out of the wilderness
of slavery into the land of freedom."

Deep River is one of the best known of the "spirituals" as
it is one of the most touching.

Deep River

Negro Spiritual

Deep _____ Riv - er, my home is o - ver
Jor - dan, _____ Deep _____ Riv - er, Lord, I
want to cross o - ver in - to camp-ground.

This song was first transcribed for the piano by the most
notable of negro composers, Coleridge-Taylor (1875-1912), who
has also arranged with fine musical instinct, a number of other
spirituals.*

Twenty-four Negro Melodies, Transcribed for the Piano, in The Musicians Library.

Not only is the negro a natural maker of melodies; he is also remarkably gifted in producing rich harmonies to go with his tunes. Few races possess this ability to such a degree. It is a well-known fact that if you give a simple melody to a group of negro singers, although they may not know a single rule of harmony, they will instinctively sing it in several parts, each one of which brings out remarkably the harmonic beauties of the song. In their own music, a solo voice usually begins with the air and at a certain point the other voices come in, each in its own way.

Many composers have made use of negro music on which to base their own works, but it was Dvořák, as we have seen, who first attracted world-wide attention to the beauty of the negro idiom by his *New World Symphony*, and his string quartet, Op. 96 and quintet, Op. 97.

Olin Downes says that "no white American save possibly Stephen C. Foster (1826-1864), in his best songs has equalled the profound feeling and the mystical inspiration of these outpourings of the soul of a race." Foster was of Southern descent. He had been with the negroes in their natural surroundings; he knew intimately the "cotton fields" and the "log cabins" which enabled him to picture, better than any other composer, the life and emotion of the negro. His songs are so numerous that we cannot even list them all here. But a few of them—*Swanee River* (*Old Folks at Home*), *My Old Kentucky Home, Old Black Joe, Massa's In De Cold, Cold Ground* and *Uncle Ned*—touch such a deep, true note that they are known and loved in almost every country of the civilized world.

The wealth of musical material to be found in negro songs has encouraged some composers to make a study of Indian music as well. In some ways the results have been disappointing. The hope that Indian music might share with negro music the distinction of being treated as American folksong seems to be thoroughly demolished; for American folksong must have a definite appeal to all Americans, while Indian music has not found much of a welcome except among the Indians themselves.

What we have learned about Aboriginal music, however, is interesting for its own sake. We find that the American Indian, like most savages, did not distinguish very sharply between dance and song. Most of the poetry which he sang was poetry with a story idea behind it. And when he sang, he interpreted the story in gesture, pantomime and rhythmic dance; not for the entertainment of an audience, by the way, but simply to express his innermost feelings. Thus Indian music is neither wholly folksong nor wholly folk-dance; but the dance element is usually important enough to give the music a strongly developed rhythm. The melodies, on the other hand, are as a rule comparatively simple, like the following Pawnee *Song of Rejoicing and Thanksgiving*. It means: "O Father, while giving thanks I wish that all good gifts may be renewed."

Kisaka*
Woman's Song of Rejoicing

For tune the Indian has most frequently used instruments generally similar to the flute, the flageolet and pan-pipes, and sometimes a crude type of harp; for rhythm he has, of course, employed the drum, usually in combination with rattles. The favorite of all appears to have been the flute.

Unlike negro songs Indian music is not harmonized; nor do the Indians themselves show any tendency to sing in separate parts. Soprano voices, alto voices, tenor voices and bass voices all sing the same notes in unison, though of course in different octaves. Sometimes when many Indians are singing together the

*See *The Indians' Book*, edited by Natalie Curtis. Published by Harper & Brothers. This song was contributed by an Indian.

different qualities of tone and the fact that some voices are high and others low, make it seem to the untrained ear that there are separate parts in harmony; it is difficult to realize that the whole song is being performed in unison. But the fact remains that Indian music is unharmonic, and for this reason it is likely always to fall short of the popularity of negro music, which lends itself so readily to four-part singing.

As to the value of Indian music to American composers, we find that Indian themes have been used occasionally. Arthur Farwell has made them the foundation of some piano compositions. Charles W. Cadman has produced several graceful lyrics on Indian themes; but it must be admitted that the finished composition in each case depends for its beauty on Cadman rather than on the original theme. The same is true of MacDowell's *Indian Suite* for orchestra, probably the most noteworthy adaptation of Indian song. The *Suite* is good because of MacDowell's genius, not because of any special beauty in the Indian music.

Frederick Jacobi, too, has written a suite for orchestra based on the ritualistic dances which still take place among the Pueblos and Navajos of New Mexico and Arizona. It is very interesting and in parts lovely, but Indian music seems too intensely racial to be representative of all the American peoples. It is the outgrowth of a life of which we can never be a part—of a country which vanished with our coming.

In our search then for something on which to base real American music, we have little to gain from the Indian. The negro, on the contrary, has given us a valuable interpretation of America. His folksongs are musically beautiful; they are something that most of us can understand and appreciate. Yet the fact that we all enjoy negro music does not mean that it is a form of musical expression natural and spontaneous with the American people as a whole. Only the negro expresses himself in just that way. The descendant of a Mayflower Pilgrim would sing in quite a different vein; the twentieth-century immigrant from Southern Europe would sing differently again. Yet these are both Americans.

For a time at least, while the American people is made up of so many unlike groups of various races, and with various traditions, we shall not have a national American music in the same sense that the Russians have a national Russian music. That is, we shall not have any definite and characteristic form of musical expression common to the whole people. But in another sense we can have a really typical American music, which attempts to interpret not the emotions of Americans, but the spirit of America itself. The youth and strength of a new land, the unshaken courage and hope of the pioneer, the joy of freedom, the shifting colors of a wide democracy—cannot fail to impress themselves strongly on the music that we create.

Nor shall we lack composers to express that spirit. Already we can count many Americans who have made their mark in music, a number of them winning far more than local reputation and not a few international fame. And their works, especially in the large orchestral forms, chamber music, and choruses with orchestral accompaniment, have almost all been produced since the close of the Civil War, a very short period indeed when compared with the centuries during which European nations have been creating music. It speaks volumes for the native ability and sturdy industry of American composers, that in scarcely more than half a century they have won a high place in the field of composition and also of teaching.

General interest in music is being stimulated by the courses in music which are given in Public Schools and Colleges. School orchestras and Glee Clubs are receiving more encouragement yearly. The competitions which take place during Music Week arouse student musicians to their highest efforts. The radio brings the best music in concerts, and brings lectures on understanding of music to any who wish to listen. All this is having a vast influence on the development of our music, and with a national atmosphere rich in natural poetry and splendid tradition, we may look hopefully to the future, confident in America's power to bring forth a distinctive music of strength and beauty unexcelled.

The following phonograph records may be used to illustrate some of the musical selections in this chapter.

Title	Victor Record No.
MUSIC OF EARLY AMERICAN COMPOSERS (American Society of Ancient Instruments).	M215, 216

Title	Victor Record No.
FROM AN INDIAN LODGE (MacDowell)—Victor Symphony Orchestra.	20342
TO A WATER-LILY (MacDowell)—Chicago Symphony Orchestra.	1152
NOBODY KNOWS THE TROUBLE I SEE—Robeson.	20068
SUNRISE CALL (Indian)—Chief Caupolican.	20983
DEEP RIVER (Burleigh)—Robeson.	20793
GOIN' HOME (Dvořák-Fisher)—Eveready Hour Group.	35823
STEPHEN FOSTER MELODIES—Shilkret-Victor Orchestra.	9246-9249

INDIAN THEMES MADE ON INDIAN FLUTES.

BY THE WATERS OF THE MINNETONKA	Lieurance	⎫
WINNEBAGO LOVE SONG	Lieurance	⎪
LOVE WITH TEARS (Cheyenne)	Lieurance	⎬ 21972
PUEBLO LULLABY	Lieurance	⎪
OMAHA CEREMONIAL	Lieurance	⎭

CONCERTO GROSSO (Bloch)—Philadelphia Chamber Sinfonietta.	
SHEEP AND GOAT (Walkin' to the Pasture) (Guion)—Eaver.	24532
CHANT OF THE SNAKE DANCERS (Hopi).	24783A
SKYSCRAPERS (Carpenter)—Victor Symphony Orchestra.	11250-11252
THE KING'S HENCHMAN (Taylor)—Tibbett—Metropolitan Opera Chorus.	8103
TURKEY IN THE STRAW (Guion)—Victor Concert Orchestra.	22131

QUESTIONS

1. Tell briefly what influences interfered with the progress of American music during the seventeenth and eighteenth centuries.

2. Mention at least six persons or events important in American musical development between 1700 and 1850.

3. Name one great singing society organized during the nineteenth century. Name three important orchestras organized during the same century. Give the approximate dates of each.

4. Tell what you know of Edward MacDowell's importance in American music.

5. Compare *Deep River* with the Indian melody given in this chapter. Which has the more appealing tune? Which has the sharper rhythm? Which, on the whole strikes you as being more musical?

6. Discuss briefly any modern influences which you think likely to make music more generally appreciated here in America.

HISTORY, WITH CONTEMPORANEOUS CHRONOLOGICAL TABLE OF EVENTS IN MUSICAL HISTORICAL EVENTS

B. C.	MUSICAL EVENTS	CONTEMPORARY EVENTS
5000	The ravanostron, ancestor of the violin, was invented in India at about this date. Chapter II.	
1000	Homeric poems are thought to have been composed at about this date. They were chanted by traveling minstrels. Chapter II.	*inefficiency*
800		The building of Carthage begun.
753		The building of Rome begun.
520	Hebrews introduced custom of singing in temples to accompaniment of instruments. Psalms collected for this purpose. Chapter II.	
500	About this time in Greece, rooms were rented for chorus practice. Chapter II.	
300	Development in India of musical drama bearing certain traits of modern opera. Chapter II.	
A. D.		
312		Constantine the Great became Emperor.
333	*no* St. Ambrose born. Chapter IV.	
410		The Visigoths captured Rome.
553		Goths expelled from Italy by Justinian. Plague raged in Rome.

A.D.	MUSICAL EVENTS	CONTEMPORARY EVENTS
590	Accession of Pope Gregory who arranged Gregorian chant. Chapter IV.	
814	Lament written on death of Charlemagne—one of oldest examples of European music that has been preserved. Chapter III.	
1095		The First Crusade. *Force?*
1147		The Second Crusade.
1157	Châtelain de Coucy born. Chapter III.	
1189		The Third Crusade.
1192	Châtelain de Coucy died. Chapter III.	
1202		The Fourth Crusade.
1204		Capture of Constantinople by the Latins.
1215		Magna Charta signed in England.
1226		St. Francis of Assisi, leader of Franciscans, died.
1228	(about) Melody of *We Won't go Home Until Morning* became popular. Chapter I.	Frederick II embarked upon the Sixth Crusade and acquired Jerusalem.
1285	*Le jeu de Robin et Marion* before the Court of the King of Naples. This musical play is considered by some to be the first Opera. Chapter III.	
1287	(about) Adam de la Halle died.	

A. D.	MUSICAL EVENTS	CONTEMPORARY EVENTS
1293		Roger Bacon, the prophet of experimental science, died.
1423		Earliest dated print.
1425	School of the Netherlands came into prominence. Chapter IV.	
1453		Hundred Years' War ends. Ottoman Turks took Constantinople.
1473		First book printed in England.
1475	Mastersingers flourished in Germany. Chapter III.	Michelangelo born.
1483	Martin Luther born. Chapter IV.	Raphael born.
1486		First ship rounded Cape of Good Hope.
1492		Columbus crossed the Atlantic to America.
1494	Hans Sachs born. Chapter IV.	
1509		Henry VIII, King of England, began his reign.
1526	(about) Palestrina born. Chapter IV.	
1545	Council of Trent. Chapter IV.	
1546	Luther died. Chapter IV.	
1560	Peri born. Chapter VII.	
1564		Shakespeare born.
1568	Claudio Monteverde born. Chapter VII.	
1576	Hans Sachs died. Chapter IV.	
1594	Performance of the opera *Dafne* at Florence. Chapter VIII. Palestrina died.	
1599		Oliver Cromwell born.

151

A.D.	MUSICAL EVENTS	CONTEMPORARY EVENTS
1600	Peri's *Euridice* first performed. Chapter VII.	
1600	(about) Francesco Cavalli born. Chapter VII.	
1609		Hudson River and Lake Champlain discovered.
1620		Mayflower expedition founded Plymouth, Mass.
1625	Peri died. Chapter VII.	
1630		Boston, Mass. founded.
1633	Lully born. Chapter VII.	
1637	Opening in Venice of the Teatro San Cassiano, the first opera-house. Chapter VII.	
1638		Harvard College founded.
1640	*Bay Psalm Book* published in Cambridge, Mass. With the exception of a trivial almanac, this was the first book printed in the Colonies. Chapter X.	
1641		Long Parliament in England.
1642		Newton born. Civil War in England.
1643	Monteverde died. Chapter VII.	Louis XIV, King of France, began his reign of 72 years.
1649		Charles I beheaded; Commonwealth in England.
1650		Puritanism attained its greatest power in England.
1658	Purcell born. Chapter V.	Cromwell died.
1659	Alessandro Scarlatti born. Chapter VII.	
1674		New Amsterdam finally became British by treaty and was renamed New York.

1676	Cavalli died. Chapter VII.	
1685	Bach born. Chapter V. Handel born. Chapter V.	James II, King of England, began his reign.
1686	Porpora born. Chapter VII.	
1687	Lully died. Chapter VII.	
1713	The first pipe-organ in a New England church was installed in King's Chapel, Boston. Chapter X.	Frederick the Great of Prussia born.
1714	Gluck born. Chapter VII.	George I, King of England, began his reign.
1717	(about) A singing school was established in Boston. Chapter X.	
1718	Handel took up residence in England. Chapter V.	
1722	Bach's *Well-Tempered Clavichord* published. Chapter V.	
1725	Alessandro Scarlatti died. Chapter VII.	
1729	Bach's *St. Matthew Passion* produced. Chapter V.	
1731	Handel's first English oratorio produced. Chapter V.	
1732	Haydn born. Chapter VI.	George Washington born.
1737	Francis Hopkinson born. Chapter X.	
1740		Frederick the Great of Prussia, began his reign.
1742	Handel's *Messiah* first performance. Chapter V.	
1746	William Billings born. Chapter X.	
1749		Goethe born.

A. D.	MUSICAL EVENTS	CONTEMPORARY EVENTS
1750	Bach died. Chapter V.	
1755		Britain and France struggled for America and India. France in alliance with Austria and Russia against Prussia and Britain (1756-1763) ; the Seven Years' War.
1756	Mozart born. Chapter VI.	
1756	A Concert Hall was built in Boston. Chapter X.	
1759	Death of Handel. Chapter V. Haydn's first symphony written. Chapter VI.	The British took Quebec.
1760		George III, King of England, began his reign.
1766	Porpora died. Chapter VII.	
1767	Gluck's *Alceste* composed. Chapter VII.	
1769		Napoleon Bonaparte born.
1770	Beethoven born. Chapter VIII.	Wadsworth born.
1773	A band was formed which gave concerts in Faneuil Hall, Boston. Chapter X.	Boston Tea Party.
1775		Revolutionary War began.
1776		Declaration of Independence by the United States.
1779	Gluck's *Iphigénie en Tauride* produced. Chapter VII.	

A.D.	MUSICAL EVENTS	CONTEMPORARY EVENTS
1783		Treaty of Peace between Britain and the United States.
1786	Mozart's *Figaro* produced. Chapter VI.	
1787	Gluck died. Mozart's *Don Giovanni* produced. Chapter VI.	The Constitutional Convention of Philadelphia set up the Federal Government of the United States.
1788	Mozart's last three symphonies written. Chapter VI.	First Federal Congress of the United States at New York.
1789		French Revolution begins.
1791	Mozart's *Magic Flute* produced. Chapter VI. Mozart died. Chapter VI. Hopkinson died. Chapter X.	
1792	Lowell Mason born. Chapter X.	France declared war on Austria. Prussia declared war on France.
1797	Schubert born. Chapter VIII.	France became a Republic.
1798	Donizetti born. Chapter VII. "Philharmonic Society" formed in Boston. Chapter X.	Bonaparte went to Egypt.
1800	William Billings died. Chapter X.	
1802	Bellini born. Chapter VII.	Victor Hugo born.
1803	Glinka born. Chapter IX.	Emerson born. Louisiana purchased from France.
1809	Haydn died. Chapter VI. Mendelssohn born. Chapter VIII.	

155

A.D.	MUSICAL EVENTS	CONTEMPORARY EVENTS
1810	Schumann born. Chapter VIII. Chopin born. Chapter VIII.	
1811	Liszt born. Chapter VIII.	Thackeray born.
1813	Verdi born. Chapter VII. Wagner born. Chapter VII.	
1815	*Handel and Haydn* Society organized in Boston. Chapter X.	Bismarck born.
1816	Rossini's *Barber of Seville* composed. Chapter VII.	
1818	Gounod born. Chapter VII.	
1821	Schubert's *Erlking* first sung in public. Chapter VIII.	Bonaparte and Keats died.
1822	César Franck born. Chapter IX.	Shelley and Herschel died.
1824	Beethoven's *Ninth Symphony* produced. Chapter VIII.	Charles X, King of France, began his reign.
1826	Stephen C. Foster born. Chapter X.	
1827	Beethoven died. Chapter VIII.	
1828	Schubert died. Chapter VIII.	
1829	William Mason born. Chapter X.	Greece independent.
1830	Anton Rubinstein born. Chapter IX.	July Revolution in France. William IV, King of England, began his reign.
1831	Bellini's *La Sonnambula* produced. Chapter VII.	
1833	Brahms born. Chapter IX. The *Academy of Music* founded in Boston. Chapter X.	
1835	Theodore Thomas born. Chapter X. First performance of Donizetti's *Lucia di Lammermoor*. Chapter VII. Bellini died. Chapter VII. Moussorgsky born. Chapter IX.	The word *socialism* first used.

156

A. D.	MUSICAL EVENTS	CONTEMPORARY EVENTS
1835	Saint-Saëns born. **Chapters VIII** and IX.	
1836	Glinka's *A Life for the Czar* produced—first Russian opera. Chapter IX.	
1837		Victoria, Queen of England, began her reign.
1838	Bizet born. Chapter VII.	
1839	Moussorgsky born. Chapter IX. Dudley Buck born. Chapter X.	
1840	Peter Tchaïkovsky born. Chapter IX.	Queen Victoria married Prince Albert of Saxe-Coburg-Gotha.
1841	Anton Dvořák born. Chapters IX and X.	
1842	Arthur Sullivan born. Chapter IX.	
1843	Edvard Grieg born. Chapter IX.	
1844	Rimsky-Korsakov born. Chapter IX.	
1846	William Gilchrist born. Chapter X.	War between United States and Mexico.
1847	Mendelssohn died. **Chapter VIII.**	
1848	Frederick Gleason born. Chapter X.	Louis Philippe, King of France, deposed; second French Republic established.
1849	Chopin died. Chapter VIII.	Discovery of gold in California.
1852		Napoleon III, Emperor of France, began his reign.
1853	Verdi's *Il Trovatore* produced. Chapter VII. Arthur Foote born. Chapter X.	
1856	George W. Chadwick born. Chapter X.	Crimean War began.

A. D.	MUSICAL EVENTS	CONTEMPORARY EVENTS
1856	Schumann died. Chapter VIII.	Alexander II, Czar of Russia, began his reign.
1857	Glinka died. Chapter IX. Edward Elgar born. Chapter IX.	*Dred Scott* case decided in United States.
1858	Puccini born. Chapter IX.	
1859	Gounod's *Faust* produced. Chapter VII.	Victor Emmanuel, first King of Italy, began his reign.
		Abraham Lincoln became President of the United States.
1861	MacDowell born. Chapter X.	Civil War began in United States.
1862	Debussy born. Chapter IX.	
1863	Horatio Parker born. Chapter X.	
1864	Richard Strauss born. Chapter IX.	
1865	Wagner's *Tristan and Isolde* first produced. Chapter VII. Sibelius born. Chapter IX.	Surrender of Lee's Army.
1867	Mrs. H. H. A. Beach born. Chapter X.	
1868	Wagner's *Die Meistersinger* produced. Chapter VII.	Japan opened to the world.
1869	Charpentier born.	
1870		Franco-Prussian War.
1871	Frederick S. Converse born. Chapter X.	Paris surrendered (January.) King of Prussia became German Emperor. The Peace of Frankfort.
1872	Vaughn Williams and Scriabin born. Chapter IX.	
1873	Sergei Rachmaninoff born. Chapter IX.	

158

1875   Bizet died. **Chapter VII.**
        Coleridge-Taylor and Ravel born.
        Chapter IX.

1878   The Treaty of Berlin.

                                            The Armed Peace of forty-six years began in western Europe.

1879   Cyril Scott and Respighi born. Chapter IX.

1881   First performance by Boston Sym-   Garfield, President of U. S.
        phony Orchestra. Chapter X.   assassinated.
        Moussorgsky died. Chapter IX.

1882   Percy Grainger born. Chapter IX.

1883   Wagner died. Chapter VII.

1885   Sullivan's *Mikado* produced. Chap-   U. S. Grant died.
        ter IX.

1886   Liszt died. Chapter VIII.

1887   Verdi's *Othello* produced. Chapter VII.

1890   César Franck died. Chapter IX.

1891   Prokofieff born.

1892   Honegger born.

1893   Gounod died. Chapter VII.
        Tchaïkovsky died. Chapter IX.
        Dvořák's *New World Symphony* first performed. Chapter IX.
        Goossens born. Chapter IX.

1894   Rubinstein died. Chapter IX.   R. L. Stevenson died.

1897   Puccini's *La Bohême* produced.
        Brahms died. Chapter IX.

1900   Arthur Sullivan died. Chapter IX.
        Puccini's *Tosca* produced. Chapter IX.

A. D.	MUSICAL EVENTS	CONTEMPORARY EVENTS
1901	Verdi died. Chapter VII.	Queen Victoria died; Edward VII began reign in England.
1902	Debussy's *Pelléas et Mélisande* produced. Chapter IX.	
1904	Anton Dvořák died. Chapter IX and X.	Russo-Japanese War
1905	Puccini's *Madame Butterfly* produced. Chapter IX.	
1907	Grieg died. Chapter IX.	
1908	MacDowell died. Chapter X. Rimsky-Korsakov died. Chapter IX.	
1912	Massenet died. Chapter VII. Coleridge-Taylor died. Chapter IX.	China became a Republic.
1914		Great War in Europe began.
1917		U. S. entered World War. Establishment of Bolshevik régime in Russia.
1918		The Armistice.
1919	Horatio Parker died, Dec. 18. Chapter X.	
1920	Debussy died. Chapter IX.	First meeting of the League of Nations.
1921	Saint-Saëns died. Chapter IX.	Greeks made war on the Turks.
1922		Defeat of the Greeks by Turks.
1923		French invasion of Germany.
1924	Puccini died. Chapter IX.	Evacuation of Germany by Allied Armies of Occupation.
1930		
1931	Chadwick died. Chapter X.	
1934	Elgar, Delius, and Holst died.	

INDEX

INDEX

INDEX